I Don't Wanna Cook Cook Book

FOREWORD

Welcome to my cook book. I hope you will enjoy these recipes as much as my husband and I do. The recipes in this book have been created by Erik or myself, or have been gathered from friends and family from over the years. We have cooked each and every recipe in this book, and have found them to be easy or fairly easy to make, and have a wonderful taste. The aroma that fills our home is a plus as well.

Over the years I have read many a cook book, and still love to peruse new ones when time allows. I wanted to design a cook book that is easy to read, as well as recipes that are easy to make. Something that one could grab off the shelf, find the index, flip to the recipe, and get your meal started to help in freeing up time for rest and relaxation. Hence the title of the book: "I Don't Wanna Cook – Cook Book".

My wish is for my cook book to find a spot in your kitchen that will be an everyday go to in preparing your family's daily meals.

May you have fun with each and every recipe, and smile when dinner is ready!

ENJOY!

From my kitchen, to yours,
Eric Drain

STRESS PREVENTION

STRESS PREVENTION

- Don't schedule meetings at times of the day when you know that you don't function well. If you function best in the afternoon, don't set potentially stressful meetings with your boss or co-workers in the morning.
- Take coffee breaks – and use them to relax and clear your mind.
- Take five minutes relaxation breaks each morning and afternoon. Use them to think of peaceful things and use your favorite relaxation technique.
- Leave for work 15 minutes earlier than usual to avoid the stress of heavy traffic and drive slower than usual. Take a different route and focus on your surroundings.
- Put notes on your calendar and telephone at work reminding you to relax at specific times throughout the day.
- Allow yourself distractions. Hang a picture of a peaceful setting on your office wall and indulge yourself in daydreaming about it for a few minutes.
- Take time off regularly. It'll keep you relaxed.
- Make sure you maintain a regular schedule. Go to bed and get up at roughly the same time each day. This gets your body into a regular rhythm.
- Be aware that alcohol, medications and coffee can all interfere with sleeping and resting patterns and habits.
- Get regular exercise every morning or afternoon. Exercising at night will delay sleep.
- Try home remedies, including things like a hot bath or glass of warm milk when you can't sleep.
- Make a "to do" list (add and remove as you go).

TIPS

DRAIN CLEANER

1 gallon, boiling Water
1 cup, salt
1 cup, apple cider vinegar
¼ cup, baking soda

Mix ingredients, let foam, pour down drain.

- This is a method that my grandmother utilized in each drain of her house each month for years to keep her drains clog free.

MEASUREMENT CONVERSION CHART

LIQUID MEASURE

8 ounces =	1 cup
2 cups =	1 pint
16 ounces =	1 pint
4 cups =	1 quart
1 gill =	½ cup
	or ¼ pint
2 pints =	1 quart
4 quarts =	1 gallon
31.5 gallon =	1 barrel
3 tsp =	1 tbsp
2 tbsp =	1/8 cup
	or 1 fluid ounce
4 tbsp =	¼ cup
8 tbsp =	½ cup
1 pinch =	1/8 tsp or less
1 tsp =	60 drops

DRY MEASURE

2 pints	= 1 quart
4 quarts	= 1 gallon
8 quarts	= 2 gallons
	or 1 peck
4 pecks	= 8 gallons
	1 bushel
16 ounces	= 1 pound

US DRY TO METRIC

.0353 ounces	= 1 gram
¼ ounce	= 7 grams
1 ounce	= 28.35 grams
4 ounces	= 113.4 grams
8 ounces	= 226.8 grams
1 pound	= 454 grams

US LIQUID TO METRIC

1 fluid oz.	=	29.573 milliliters
1 cup	=	230 milliliters
1 quart	=	.94635 liters
1 gallon	=	3.7854 liters
.033814 Fluid ounce	=	1 milliliter
3.3814 Fluid ounce	=	1 deciliter
33.814 Fluid ounce	=	1 liter
1.0567 Quarts	=	1 liter

SUBSTITUTIONS

Allspice	1 tsp	½ tsp cinnamon, ¼ tsp ginger, and ¼ tsp cloves.
Baking Mix	1 cup	1 cup pancake mix.
Banking Powder	1 tsp	¼ tsp baking soda, ½ tsp Cream of tartar.
Beer	1 cup	1 cup chicken broth.
Brandy	¼ cup	1 tsp imitation brandy Extract plus enough water to make ¼ cup.
Bread Crumbs	1 cup	1 cup cracker crumbs.
Broth: Chix or Beef	1 cup	1 bouillon cube, 1 cup boiling water.
Brown Sugar	1 cup, pkd	1 cup white sugar, ¼ cup molasses.
Butter (Salted)	1 cup	7/8 cup vegetable oil.
Butter (Unsalted)	1 cup	7/8 cup vegetable oil.
Buttermilk	1 cup	1 cup yogurt.
Cheddar Cheese	1 cup	1 cup shredded Colby Cheddar.
Chicken Base	1 tbsp	1 cup chicken broth or stock.
Chocolate (semi-swt)	1 oz	1 ounce semi-sweet Chocolate chips, 1 tsp shortening.
Chocolate (non-swt)	1 oz	3 tbsp cocoa, 1 tbsp shortening.
Cocoa	¼ cup	1 ounce square unsweetened chocolate.
Cream of Mushroom Soup	10.75 oz	10.75 ounce can condensed cream of celery, Chicken, or golden mushroom soup.
Corn Syrup	1 cup	1 cup honey.

Cottage Cheese	1 cup	1 cup ricotta cheese.
Cracker Crumbs	1 cup	1 cup ground oats.
Cream (half and half)	1 cup	7/8 cup milk, 1 tbsp butter.
Cream (heavy)	1 cup	¾ cup milk, 1/3 cup butter.
Cream (light)	1 cup	¾ cup milk, 3 tbsp butter.
Cream (whipped)	1 cup	1 cup frozen whipped TPNG
Cream Cheese	1 cup	1 cup pureed cottage cheese.
Cream of Tartar	1 tsp	2 tsp lemon juice or vinegar.
Egg	1 ea	3 tbsp mayonnaise.
Evaporated Milk	1 cup	1 cup light cream.
Fats for Baking	1 cup	1 cup applesauce.
Flour-Self Rising	1 cup	7/8 cup all purpose flour, 1-1/2 Tbsp baking powder, ½ tsp salt.
Garlic	1 clove	½ tsp garlic salt.
Gelatin	1 tbsp	2 tsp agar
Ginger-dry	1 tsp	2 tsp chopped fresh ginger.
Ginger-fresh	1 tsp minced	½ tsp ground dried ginger.
Green Onion	½ cup	½ cup chopped onion.
Hazelnuts	1 cup	1 cup almonds
Herbs-fresh	1 tbsp	1 tsp dried herbs.
Herring	8 ounces	8 ounces of sardines.
Honey	1 cup	1-1/4 cup white sugar, 1/3 Cup water.
Hot Pepper Sauce	1 tsp	¾ tsp cayenne pepper, 1 tsp vinegar.
Ketchup	1 cup	1 cup tomato sauce, 1 tsp vinegar, 1 tbsp sugar.
Lard	1 cup	1 cup butter.
Lemon Grass	2 stalks	1 tbsp lemon zest.
Lemon Juice	1 tsp	½ tsp vinegar.
Lemon Zest	1 tsp	2 tbsp Lemon Juice.
Lime Juice	1 tsp	1 tsp vinegar.
Lime Zest	1 tsp	1 tsp lemon zest.

Macadamia Nuts	1 cup	1 cup almonds.
Mace	1 tsp	1 tsp nutmeg.
Margarine	1 cup	7/8 cup vegetable oil, ½ tsp salt.
Mayonnaise	1 cup	1 cup sour cream.
Milk-whole	1 cup	1 cup water or juice.
Mint-fresh	¼ cup	1 tbsp dried mint leaves.
Molasses	1 cup	Mix ¾ cup brown sugar, 1 tsp cream of tartar.
Mustard-prepared	1 tbsp	Mix together 1 tbsp dried mustard, 1 tsp water, 1 tsp vinegar, and 1 tsp sugar.
Onion	1 cup	¼ cup onion powder.
Orange Juice	1 tbsp	1 tbsp other citrus juice.
Orange Zest	1 tbsp	1 tsp lemon juice.
Parmesan Cheese	½ cup	½ cup grated Romano cheese.
Parsley	1 tbsp	1 tbsp chervil.
Pepperoni	1 ounce	1 ounce salami.
Raisin	1 cup	1 cup chopped pitted prunes.
Rice-white	1 cup, cooked	1 cup cooked brown rice.
Ricotta Cheese	1 cup	1 cup cottage cheese.
Rum	1 tbsp	½ tsp rum extract, 1 tbsp water.
Saffron	¼ tsp	¼ tsp turmeric.
Salami	1 ounce	1 ounce pepperoni.
Semi-Swt Choc Cps	1 cup	1 cup chopped nuts
Shallots, chopped	½ cup	½ cup chopped onion.
Shortening	1 cup	1 cup butter.
Sour Cream	1 cup	1 tbsp vinegar, 1 cup cream.
Sour Milk	1 cup	1 tbsp vinegar, 1 cup milk. Let stand 5 minutes.
Soy Sauce	½ cup	¼ cup Worcestershire sauce, 1 tbsp water.

Stock (beef/chix)	1 cup	1 cube beef or chicken Bouillon dissolved in 1 cup water.
Sweet Cond. Milk	14 ounce	¾ cup white sugar mixed With ½ cup water and 1-1/8 cup dry powdered milk; bring to a boil and cook, stirring frequently, until thickened, 20 minutes.
Vegetable Oil (bake)	1 cup	1 cup applesauce.
Vegetable Oil (fry)	1 cup	1 cup lard.
Vinegar	1 tsp	1 tsp lemon or lime juice.
White Sugar	1 cup	¾ cup honey.
Wine	1 cup	1 cup water.
Yeast-active dry	.25 ounce	1 cake compressed yeast.
Yogurt	1 cup	1 cup sour cream or buttermilk.

BEVERAGES

APPLE PIE MOONSHINE

½ gallon, pasteurized apple juice
½ gallon, apple cider
1 ½ cup, granulated Sugar
½ cup, dark brown sugar
4 each, cinnamon sticks
1 can, sliced apples (in fruit juice)
2 cups, 190 proof Everclear
¼ cup, fireball liqueur

- Serves 10

Add apple juice, cider, sugars and cinnamon sticks to a good stock pan; and bring to a boil, keeping it covered, and let simmer 30 minutes.
Take off heat, leaving cover on, and let cool down, should take 4 to 6 hours. Stir in 190 proof Everclear and fireball. Put 1 apple slice in each jar (I use pint jars), then strain through a cheesecloth or coffee filter and fill the jars and seal with lid.

This is best after it has aged for a couple of months. Pint jars make perfect sizes for gifts.

Enjoy!

CRAN-ORANGE DRINK

4 cups, Cran-apple drink
1 cup, orange juice
¼ cup, lemon juice
28oz bottle, carbonated water

- Make some extra for ice cubes in juices.

Mix all ingredients together; chill in refrigerator for 3 hours.

CREMORA HOT COCOA MIX

1 large bowl

2 cups, Cremora Non-Dairy Creamer
2 cups, non-fat dry milk
2 cups, sugar
1 cup, unsweetened cocoa powder

- Optional; 1 cup Instant coffee granules (for Mocha).

Combine all ingredients in large bowl. Mix well. Keep in airtight container. Use ¼ cup mix to ¾ or 1 cup boiling water.

Mix and ENJOY!

GLOGG SWEDISH NOG

6 large, eggs
¼ cup, sugar
¼ tsp, ground Cardamom
¼ tsp, ground cinnamon
¼ tsp, ground cloves
1 qt, vanilla ice cream, softened
6 cups, orange juice
¼ cup, lemon juice
1 qt, ginger ale, chilled

- Optional: Ice ring, ground nutmeg, and stick of cinnamon.

Beat eggs on low speed with mixer until blended. Add sugar and spices. Beat at medium speed until sugar is dissolved. On low speed, beat in softened ice cream. Add the juices. Cover and chill. To serve, pour the ice cream mixture into a large punch bowl. Slowly pour in ginger ale, stirring slowly. Add ice ring to punch bowl, if desired. Sprinkle nutmeg atop and add a stick of cinnamon per glass, if desired.

Ice Ring: Arrange orange slices in bottom of a small ring mold. Fill with cold water. Freeze until firm. Unmold onto plate; slip ring gently into punch bowl.

MOM'S HOT CHOCOLATE

8 quarts, non-fat dry milk
28oz, Coffee-Mate
2 lbs, dry Nestle Quick
1 lb, powered sugar

Mix all ingredients into large container, and store in cool dry place. Add mixture (to taste) to hot water.

PASSION SLUSH

1 can, frozen lemonade
10oz, strawberry daiquiri mixer
1 lb bag, frozen strawberries
46oz can pineapple juice
1 bottle, Passion Fruit Vodka
2 liter, 7-up

Mix well in large bowl. Freeze for 24 hours. Add 2/3 slush to 1/3 7-up.

Serve and drink!

POKENO SLUSH

2 cans, frozen lemonade
1 can, frozen orange juice
2 cups, strong tea
1 ½ cup, sugar
2 cups, rum, vodka, or brandy
7 cups, boiling water
2 liter, 7-up or ginger ale

Mix all ingredients. Freeze until slushy or hard. Add 7-up or ginger ale to make desired slush consistency in glass.

Drink happy. Drink at home!

RASPBERRY SLUSH

7 cups, water
7 tsp, instant raspberry tea (diet)
2 cups, sugar

Bring above ingredients to a boil, adding;

1 can, frozen orange juice
2 cans, frozen cranberry juice
1 bag, frozen raspberries (pureed)
3-4 cups, raspberry vodka

Freeze for at least 24 hours.

2 liter, 7-up

Spoon frozen slush into a glass; mix with equal parts of 7-up.

Refreshing on a hot day!

BREADS

APPLE BREAD

2 cups, chopped apples
2 cups, sugar
1 cup, oil
3 each, eggs
1 tsp, baking soda
1 tsp, salt
2 tsp, vanilla
3 cups, flour, all purpose
1-1/4 cup, chopped nuts
2 each, loaf pans, 9x5

Preheat oven to 350 degrees. Grease and flour both pans. Mix all ingredients until blended well, and place even amounts into loaf pans. Bake for 60 to 90 minutes.

BLUEBERRY LEMON BREAD

1-1/2 cups, all-purpose flour
1 tsp, baking powder
¼ tsp, salt
7 Tbsp, butter, room temperature
1-1/3 cups, sugar, divided
3 each, large eggs
2 tsp, grated lemon peel
¾ cup, milk
1-1/2 cups, fresh blueberries
4 Tbsp, fresh lemon juice

Preheat oven to 300 degrees. Butter, flour and sugar an 8 x 4 inch loaf pan; set aside. Whisk together the flour, baking powder and salt in a small bowl; set aside. Using an electric mixer, cream the butter with 1 cup sugar in large bowl until mixture is light and fluffy. Add the eggs on at a time, beating well after each addition. Add the lemon peel. Slowly mix in the reserved flour mixture alternately with the milk beginning and ending with the flour mixture. Lightly coat blue berries with small amount of flour by tossing in a separate bowl. Gently fold blueberries into the batter. Pour batter in prepared loaf pan. Bake for 1 hour or until golden brown and a tooth pick inserted into center, comes out clean. Meanwhile, bring remaining 1/3 cup sugar and the lemon juice to boil in small saucepan, stirring until sugar dissolves. Keep hot for pouring. Pierce top of hot loaf several times with a long wooden pick without touching the bottom of the loaf. Slowly, pour the hot lemon mixture over the loaf in pan. Cool for 45 minutes in pan. Turn bread out of pan and cool completely on rack.

CANDY PEPPERMINT BREAD

2 cups, all-purpose flour
¼ cup, packed brown sugar
2 tsp, baking powder
½ tsp, salt
½ cup, butter
¼ cup, nuts
1 each, beaten egg
½ cup, milk

Powdered Sugar Icing:

2 cups, powdered sugar
2 Tbsp, milk
½ tsp, vanilla extract

* Pressurized red and green decorator icing (optional).
* Crushed peppermint candies (Optional).

Stir together flour, brown sugar, baking powder, and salt. Cut in the butter until mixture resembles coarse crumbs. Add nuts. Mix egg and milk. Stir into dry mixture just till moistened. On a lightly floured surface pat dough to a 10x7 inch rectangle, ½, inch thick. Cut crosswise into 1-inch strips. Twist each strip by holding both ends. Bend 1 end to form a candy cane. Place several inches apart on greased baking sheet. Bake at 425 degrees for 10 minutes or till light brown. Carefully transfer to rack. Cool. Coat each cane with Powdered Sugar Icing. Decorate, using decorator icing, cinnamon candies, or peppermint candies, as desired.

CITRUS LOAF

2 cups, all-purpose flour
¾ cup, sugar
½ tsp, salt
½ tsp, baking soda
1 beaten, egg
1 Tbsp, finely shredded orange peel
¾ cup, orange juice
¼ tsp, finely shredded lemon peel
2 Tbsp, lemon juice
2 Tbsp, cooking oil
½ cup, coarsely chopped walnuts

In mixing bowl, thoroughly stir together flour, sugar, salt, and baking soda. Combine egg, orange peel and juice, lemon peel and juice, and cooking oil. Add egg mixture to dry ingredients, stirring just till dry ingredients are moistened. Fold in nuts. Turn batter into greased 8x4 inch loaf pan. Bake in 325 degree oven for 1 hour. Cool in pan for 10 minutes; remove from pan and cool completely on wire rack. Wrap in foil and store overnight before slicing.

COCONUT CINNAMON CHERRY BREAD

2-1/2 cups, all-purpose flour
1 cup, sugar
1 tsp, baking powder
1 tsp, baking soda
1 tsp, ground cinnamon
½ tsp, salt
3 beaten, eggs
½ cup, cooking oil
½ cup, milk
2 cups, shredded carrots
1-1/3 cups, flaked coconut
½ cup, chopped Maraschino cherries
½ cup, raisins
½ cup, chopped pecans

Stir together thoroughly all-purpose flour, sugar, baking powder, baking soda, cinnamon, and salt. Combine eggs, oil, and milk; add to the flour mixture and stir just till blended. Stir in shredded carrots, coconut, Maraschino cherries, raisins, and pecans. Turn into 4 well-greased and floured 16-ounce fruit or vegetable cans. Bake at 350 degrees for 45 to 50 minutes. Remove from cans; cool thoroughly on rack. Wrap in foil; store in refrigerator.

Makes 4 small loaves.

CREAM CHEESE PEANUT BUTTER BANANA STREUSEL

¾ cup, butter, softened
8oz, package cream cheese, softened
2 cups, flour
2 each, large eggs
1-1/4 cups, un-sifted all-purpose flour
1-1/4 cups, sifted light roast peanut flour
½ tsp, baking powder
½ tsp, baking soda
½ tsp, salt
1-1/2 cups, mashed ripe bananas
1 cup, chopped salted peanuts
½ tsp, vanilla extract
Peanut Butter Streusel

Preheat oven to 375. Beat butter and cream cheese at medium speed until creamy. Gradually add sugar, beating until light and fluffy. Add eggs, 1 at a time, beating just until blended after each addition. Combine all-purpose flour and next 4 ingredients; gradually add to butter mixture, beating at low speed just until blended. Stir in bananas, peanuts, and vanilla. Spoon batter into 2 greased and floured 8x4 inch loaf pans. Sprinkle Peanut Butter Streusel over batter in pans. Bake at 375 degrees for 1 hour and 10 minutes or until a toothpick comes out clean. Shield with aluminum foil after 55 minutes to prevent excessive browning. Cool bread on wire racks for 10 minutes. Remove from pans to wire racks and cool another 30 minutes before slicing.

Peanut Butter Streusel: Combine ½ cup plus 1 Tbsp all-purpose flour and ½ cup firmly packed brown sugar in a small bowl. Cut in ¼ cup cold butter and 3 Tbsp creamy peanut butter with a fork until mixture resembles small peas.

DUTCH CHRISTMAS BREAD

5 cups, all-purpose flour
1 package, active dry yeast
1-1/4 cups, milk
½ cup, butter or margarine
¾ cup, sugar
1 tsp, salt
1 egg, beaten
¾ cup, raisins
½ cup, currants
1/3 cup, finely chopped candied citron
½ cup, finely chopped blanched almonds
Glaze

In large mixer bowl combine 2 cups of the flour and the yeast. In saucepan heat the 1-1/4 cups milk, butter or margarine, sugar, and salt just till warm and butter is almost melted. Stir into flour with the eggs. Beat at low speed for ½ minute, scraping sides of the bowl. Beat 3 minutes at high speed. Add raisins, currants, and citron; mix well. By hand, stir in enough of the remaining flour to make moderate soft dough. Turn out onto a lightly floured surface; knead 5 to 8 minutes till smooth and elastic. Place dough in a lightly greased bowl; turn once to grease surface. Cover; let rise in a warm place about 1-1/2 hours or till double. Punch down dough; turn out onto a lightly floured surface. Divide into 4 portions. Shape into 6 inch loaves. Place on greased baking sheet 3 inches apart. Cover; let rise again for about 1 hour. Bake in 375 degree oven for 30 minutes or till loaves sound hollow when lightly tapped. Cool; drizzle with glaze. Sprinkle almonds on top. Yield 4 loafs.

Glaze: Stir together 1 cup powdered sugar, ¼ tsp vanilla extract, and 2 Tbsp milk.

PRETZEL ROLLS

Dough:

7 cups, all-purpose flour
1 tsp, salt
3 Tbsp, canola oil
2 tsp, active dry yeast
2-1/2 cups, milk, slightly warmed
1 cup, water, slightly warmed
Coarse sea salt for sprinkling

Bath:

7 cups, water
1 Tbsp, salt
4 Tbsp , baking soda

In a small container, mix yeast with warm milk and let rest for 10 minutes. Whisk 5-3/4 cups of flour and 1 tsp salt in a large bowl. Add canola oil and warm water to yeast mixture. Pour into bowl of flour and salt. Knead in the bowl until dough is mostly smooth. Only add more flour if dough cannot be easily handled, it will be somewhat stiff. Cover the bowl with a dish towel and put in warm place to rise for one hour. Punch down dough and knead in bowl for one minute. Cut dough into 15 pieces. Form balls. Place on a well greased surface. Let the balls rise for 15 minutes. While the dough balls are rising, preheat oven to 400 degrees and get the pretzel bath ready. In a large pot, bring water, salt and baking soda to a rolling boil. Plunge three dough balls into the water and let them poach for 1 minute total. Using a slotted spoon, transfer them to a well greased baking sheet. Repeat process for rest of rolls. With a serrated knife, cut 2-3 lines across each roll and sprinkle with coarse sea salt. Bake for 20 to 25 minutes or until pretzels are a rich brown.

SAUSAGE BREAD

3 rolls, refrigerated pizza dough
1 lb, sausage, browned
1 lb, ground beef, browned
4 eggs, beaten
½ cup, mozzarella cheese, set aside
½ cup, parmesan cheese, set aside
1 stick, butter, melted, set aside

Preheat oven to 350 degrees. Roll dough on wax paper; add ingredients, except butter and cheeses, down center of dough and pinch closed. Bake in 350 degree oven for 30 minutes. Brush with melted butter, and sprinkle with mozzarella and parmesan cheese.

BREAKFAST

BREAKFAST CRESCENTS

8 count, crescent rolls
8 slices, bacon, cooked
5 eggs, beaten
1 cup, shredded cheddar cheese

Preheat oven to 375 degrees. Lay crescents out in star pattern, overlapping. Place bacon on each crescent. Scramble eggs and place on center part of crescents. Top with cheese, fold crescents over, and top with cheese again.

Bake at 375 degrees for 17 minutes or till golden brown.

BREAKFAST TATER TOT CASSEROLE

1 lb pre-cooked; ham, bacon, and sausage.
4 cups, shredded cheddar cheese
2 cups, milk
4 each, large eggs, beaten
2 lbs, tater tots
9x13 square pan

Preheat oven to 350 degrees. Mix milk and eggs in medium bowl.
Prepare in layers; meat, cheese, egg mixture, and tater tots.
Bake at 350 degrees for 45 minutes.

CHOCOLATE GRAVY

1 cup, granulated sugar
1 Tbsp, butter
1-1/2 cups, milk
2 Tbsp, all-purpose flour
3 Tbsp, unsweetened cocoa powder

Mix all the dry ingredients in a heavy saucepan with a whisk. Using a whisk blends everything better than a spoon. Stir in the milk. Cook over medium heat stirring constantly. Remove the pot when the mixture is thick like pudding. Add the butter. Stir in until completely melted. Serve over biscuits with a teaspoon of butter dollops on top.

CRESCENT BREAKFAST CASSEROLE

1 can of grand's crescent rolls
1 lb, sausage/hamburger, browned
1 bag, Ore-Ida Potatoes O'Brien w/onions & peppers
16oz, shredded cheddar cheese
6 eggs, beaten, mix with milk
2 cups, milk, mix with eggs

- 9x13 metal baking pan.

Set oven to 350 degrees. Grease 9x13 baking pan. Place crescent in bottom of pan. Add meat/sausage, potatoes, shredded cheese; milk and egg mixture. Cook immediately at 350 degrees for 40 to 45 minutes, or refrigerate for 24 hours, then cook.

FARMER'S CASSEROLE

3 cups, frozen hash browns (1/2 bag)
1 cup, shredded cheddar & Monterey jack cheese
1 cup, cooked & diced ham or Canadian bacon
¼ cup, sliced green onions
6 eggs, beaten (or 1 cup egg beaters)
12oz can evaporated milk
¼ Tbsp, black pepper
1/8 Tbsp, salt

Grease or spray a 2 quart baking dish, or 9x13 cake pan. Place hash browns in bottom of pan. Then, layer cheese, meat, and onion. In a medium bowl, combine eggs, milk, salt, and pepper. Pour over potatoes. You may cover and refrigerate for several hours or overnight. (Taste best this way!) Bake uncovered at 350 degrees for 40 to 45 minutes. If chilled, bake for 55 to 60 minutes.

FARMER'S DINNER

1 bag, square hash browns
2 cups, ground beef; ham; or hot dogs
2 cups, shredded cheddar cheese
6 eggs, beaten
1 Tbsp, black pepper
1 Tbsp, salt
1 large, onion, diced

Fry potatoes with onion. At ¾ done, add any kind of meat (beef, ham, hot dogs, etc.). Add eggs, black pepper, salt and cook thru. Add shredded cheddar cheese to top and cover until melted.

OVEN BAKED SWEET PECAN TOAST

8 slices, French bread, ¾ inch thick
6 eggs, beaten
1 cup, half and half
2 Tbsp, sugar
½ tsp, vanilla extract
½ tsp, cinnamon
1/8 tsp, salt
1/3 cup, butter
½ cup, pecans, chopped
½ cup, brown sugar
½ cup, butter, melted

Place bread in a single layer in a greased 9x13 glass baking dish. Blend together eggs, half and half, sugar, vanilla extract, salt and cinnamon. Pour over bread, turning bread once to coat evenly. Refrigerate overnight covered. In morning, preheat oven to 400 degrees. Place 1/3 cup butter in a 10x15" jelly roll pan. Place pan in oven to melt. Remove pan from oven and tilt to coat pan evenly with butter. Arrange soaked bread on jelly roll pan. Melt ½ cup butter; add pecans and brown sugar. Mix and spread on bread. Bake 25 minutes or until firm and golden brown.

PEANUT BUTTER AND JELLY FLAP JACKS

1 cup, sifted light roast peanut flour
1 cup, un-sifted all-purpose flour
3 Tbsp, baking powder
¼ tsp, salt
¾ cup, creamy peanut butter
¼ cup, honey
2 Tbsp, vegetable oil
2 large eggs, beaten
2 cups, milk
1 cup, strawberry preserves
Topping; favorite jelly

Process first 9 ingredients in a food processor until smooth, stopping once to scrape down sides. Pour ¼ cup batter for each flap jack onto a hot, lightly greased griddle or large nonstick skillet. Cook flap jacks 4 minutes or until edges look cooked. Turn and cook 4 minutes or until done. Microwave your favorite jelly in safe bowl for 45 seconds, stirring after 30 seconds. Spread on top of flap jacks before serving.

SKILLET MORNING CASSEROLE

1 package, sausage gravy
5 cups, tater tots
1 Tbsp, vegetable oil
½ cup, sausage, cooked and crumbled
1-1/2 cups, water
3 large eggs, beaten
1-1/2 cups, shredded cheddar cheese
1 Tbsp, chives, minced

Preheat oven to 350 degrees. Simmer oil in a 12 inch skillet.
Brown tater tots 5 minutes, remove from heat; evenly sprinkle on
sausage. Whisk gravy mix into water. Beat eggs into gravy mix.
Pour evenly over tater tots. Bake 35 minutes. Sprinkle on cheese,
bake another 5 minutes or until melted. Cut into wedges, and
garnish with chives.

WESTERN HASH BROWN CASSEROLE

1 package, hash browns, frozen
2 cups, sliced ham, thawed and cubed
½ cup, onion, diced
½ cup, green bell pepper, diced
1-1/2 cups, shredded Monterey jack cheese
12 eggs, beaten
1 cup, milk

Layer 1/3 of potatoes, ham, onions, green peppers and cheese into the bottom of a 6 quart or larger slow cooker, sprayed with cooking oil. Repeat with remaining two layers. Beat together eggs and milk. Pour mixture over the layers and cook on low 8 to 10 hours or overnight.

APPETIZERS

ARTICHOKE PEPPER DIP

14oz can, artichoke hearts, drained and chopped
4oz can, green chili peppers, rinsed, seeded, and chopped
1 cup, grated parmesan cheese
1 cup, mayonnaise or salad dressing
1 bag, tortilla chips
1 bag, breadsticks

Combine the chopped artichoke hearts, chopped chili peppers, cheese, and mayonnaise or salad dressing. Turn mixture into a 12 inch round baking dish. Bake in a 350 degree oven about 30 minutes. Serve warm with tortilla chips and breadsticks.

BLT DIP

1 cup, mayonnaise or salad dressing
1 cup, sour cream
½ lb, crumbled bacon
½ cup, tomatoes, diced
3 sleeves, crackers

Mix all ingredients in medium bowl and serve with crackers.

CHEESE BALLS

4 packs, cream cheese, softened
1 cup, green onions, chopped
4 cups, shredded cheddar cheese
4 cups, shredded Swiss cheese
4 packs, Buddig sliced beef
8 tsp, Worcestershire sauce

Mix all ingredients in a large bowl, and make into balls. This will make 4 Cheese Balls. Refrigerate for 24 hours for best taste. Serve with your favorite crackers, chips, etc.

CHILI VELVEETA DIP

1 lb, Velveeta prepared cheese
15oz can, chili w/beans
½ lb, ground beef, cooked
10oz can, Ro-Tel diced tomatoes & green chilies w/juice
1 cup, sour cream

Chop up Velveeta into squares, and add all ingredients to medium sauce pan. Heat on medium-low heat; stirring every 3-minutes, until melted and blended.

Serve with Cheese Nips, Wheat Thins, Tortilla Chips, Celery Stocks, and Carrot Sticks.

GUACAMOLE

4 each, avocados, ripe
¼ each, red onion, finely chopped
½ cup, cilantro, chopped fine
6 Tbsp, lime juice
2 tsp, kosher salt
1 each, jalapeno, seeded and finely chopped
Garlic to taste

Cut avocados in half and remove pits, and keep one. Scoop out avocados with a spoon into a medium bowl; mash. Add onions, cilantro, lime juice, salt, jalapeno and garlic salt. Press reserved pit into the guacamole to keep it from browning. Serve with Tortilla Chips.

HUMMUS

29oz can, chickpeas, drained and rinsed
1/3 cup , Tahini
½ each, zest of lemon
1 each, juice of lemon
1/3 cup , water
2 Tbsp, Evoo
¾ tsp, salt
¼ tsp, cumin
Black pepper to taste
1 garlic clove, minced (add to top)
Red pepper flakes to taste (add to top)

Mix all ingredients, excluding Garlic and Red Pepper Flakes, in Food Processor. Place on serving dish; add Garlic and Red Pepper Flakes on top.

Spread or dip with favorite snacks.

JALAPENOS, STUFFED

12 each, jalapenos
2 packs, cream cheese, softened
12 slices, bacon, uncooked

Cut jalapenos in half and remove seeds. Fill with cream cheese and wrap with 1 slice of bacon, secure with toothpicks.

Place on flat cooking sheet, heat oven to 350 degrees, cook for 20 minutes. Let cool for 15 minutes and serve.

KRISPY VEGGIE DIP

15oz can, black-eyed peas, drained
15oz can, black beans, rinsed and drained
15oz can, whole kernel corn, drained
½ cup, onion, chopped
½ cup, green pepper, chopped
4oz can, jalapeno peppers, diced
14.5oz can, tomatoes, diced and drained
1 cup, Italian dressing
½ tsp, garlic salt

Mix all ingredients together and refrigerate overnight. Serve with tortilla chips.

MEXICAN CORN DIP

1 can, Mexican corn, drained
1 cup, salad dressing
½ cup, parmesan cheese, grated
4 oz, pepper jack cheese, shredded

Mix all ingredients together and place in a greased oven safe dish.
Bake at 350 degrees for 45 minutes. Serve with corn chips.

PEANUT HUMMUS

2 cup, peanuts, shelled and boiled
1-1/2 Tbsp, parsley, chopped
4 Tbsp, peanut butter, creamy
3 Tbsp, fresh lemon juice
2 tsp, garlic, minced
1/2 tsp, ground cumin
½ tsp, red pepper
4 Tbsp, olive oil

Process first 7 ingredients in a food processor until coarsely chopped, scrape down sides as needed. With food processor running, pour olive oil through food chute in a slow, steady stream, processing until mixture is blended. Stir in 5 Tbsp water, for desired consistency.

Serve with favorite sides.

QUESO DIP

1 brick, Velveeta cheese
8oz, cream cheese
10 oz can Ro-Tel tomatoes
10 oz can, cream of mushroom soup
1 lb, ground beef

Brown ground beef, mix all ingredients into crock pot until blended and heated. Serve with your favorite snacks.

RANCH DIP

1 oz packet, ranch dip mix
1 pint, sour cream
¼ cup, bacon bits
1 cup, cheddar cheese, shredded

Mix all ingredients in serving dish. Serve with favorite chips.

ROTEL DIP

1 lb, ground beef
1 lb, ground sausage
1 large onion, finely chopped
1 lb, jalapeno cheese
1 lb, Velveeta cheese
1 can of Ro-Tel tomatoes
1 can, cream of chicken soup

Brown ground beef and ground sausage together; with onions and set aside. Melt jalapeno cheese and Velveeta; adding Ro-Tel tomatoes and cream of chicken soup, mixing well. Add meat mixture; blending well until heated thoroughly.

Serve with favorite chips or snack crackers.

SALSA DIP

2 lbs, Velveeta cheese
2 cups, chunky salsa

Cut up Velveeta cheese into squares. Add Velveeta and Salsa into medium sauce pan. Simmer stirring frequently until ingredients are well blended and heated.

Serve Tortilla chips.

SEASONED PRETZELS

2 lbs, pretzels
16oz bottle, Orville Redenbacher popcorn oil
1oz packet, hidden valley original ranch dressing
2 tsp, dill weed
1 tsp, garlic powder

Yield (2) 1 gallon ice cream buckets *

Mix together oil, dressing and seasonings. Pour over pretzels.
Shake well every few hours (or when ever you remember) until
seasonings well coated and oil mostly absorbed.

** NOTE: This makes a lot of pretzels. Find a very large
container and make sure it has a tight sealed lid!

SPICY CRACKERS

4 sleeves, premium saltines
1-1/4 cup, canola oil
½ packet, McCormick burrito seasoning
½ packet, McCormick taco seasoning
1/8 tsp, cayenne pepper

Stir spices into oil. Pour over crackers in 2 gallon Zip-lock bag. Gently toss every 10 minutes until all is absorbed (1 hour). Leave overnight. Keep stored in Tupperware container.

Spicy crackers go perfect with a cocktail or glass of wine!

TACO DIP

½ head of lettuce
½ package, shredded cheddar
1 bottle, Ortega taco sauce
½ cup, cream cheese
½ cup, sour cream
½ pack, taco seasoning

Mix taco sauce, cream cheese, sour cream, and taco seasoning in medium bowl. After all is blended, top with lettuce and shredded cheddar.

Serve with tortilla chips.

TARTAR SAUCE

½ cup, mayonnaise
1-1/2 Tbsp, onion, minced
1 Tbsp, sweet pickle relish
1-1/2 tsp, carrots, shredded
1-1/2 tsp, sugar

Mix all ingredients well in serving bowl. Serve with fish.

SALADS

APPLE SALAD

3 large , gala apples, chunk cut, w/or w/o peel
1 can, pineapple chunks, drained
1 box, instant butterscotch pudding (use dry)
1 small tub, cool whip
1-1/2 cup, nuts (whole or chopped)

Mix apples and pineapple together, put dry pudding on top, stir to mix. Add cool whip and nuts, mix until well blended, chill to serve.

BEST PASTA SALAD

1 bunch, broccoli, cut into bite size pieces
1 head, cauliflower, cut into bit size pieces
1 box, Rotelle spiral pasta, cooked al dente'
1 lb, thick bacon, cooked and crumbled

Sauce

2/3 cup, sugar
½ cup, cider vinegar
1 cup, mayo
½ cup, canola oil

Heat on medium heat, boil stirring constantly, set aside to cool.

Salad Mix

In large bowl, mix broccoli, cauliflower, Rotelle spiral pasta, and bacon together until blended. Mix in sauce mix, toss until coated. Refrigerate at least 2 hours.

BOWTIE PASTA SALAD

1 head, broccoli, cut into bit size pieces
1 head, cauliflower, cut into bite size pieces
1 box, bowtie pasta, cooked al dente' and rinsed w/cold water
2 small packets, real bacon pieces

Sauce

2/3 cup, sugar
½ cup, cider vinegar
1 cup, mayonnaise
½ cup, canola oil

Salad Mix

Mix sauce items together, heating on medium heat to boiling, stirring constantly, and set aside to cool. Toss broccoli, cauliflower, bowtie pasta, and bacon pieces until blended. Toss sauce into mix until well coated. Refrigerate for at least 2 hours.

BROCCOLI SALAD

1 head, broccoli, cut into bite size pieces
1 head, cauliflower, cut into bite size pieces
½ lb, bacon, cooked and crumbled
1 cup, shredded cheddar cheese

Sauce

1 cup, mayonnaise
1 cup, sour cream
¼ cup, sugar
½ tsp, salt

Mix sauce items together in bowl and set aside. Mix broccoli, cauliflower, bacon, and shredded cheddar together until well blended. Toss in sauce until all is well coated. Refrigerate for at least 2 hours.

CHINESE COLE SLAW

1 package, Cole slaw
1 package, ramen noodles, crushed
½ cup, slivered almonds
½ cup, sun flower seeds
¼ cup, butter

Saute' almonds and noodles in butter until brown. Add sun flower seeds, remove from heat.

Dressing

½ cup, canola oil
¼ cup, vinegar
¼ cup, sugar
1 Tbsp, soy sauce

Mix dressing ingredients together just before serving, and set aside.

Toss all ingredients together in large bowl until well blended, and serve.

CHIX SALAD

2 cups, canned chicken breast, drained
½ cup, grapes, washed and sliced in halves
1 boiled egg, chopped
½ cup, gherkins, chopped
1 Tbsp, onion, minced
¾ cup, mayonnaise
1-1/2 Tbsp, sugar

Mix all ingredients together and serve on favorite sliced bread.

COLE SLAW

1 package, Cole slaw
½ cup, mayonnaise
2 Tbsp, apple cider vinegar
1 Tbsp, milk
½ tsp, sugar
2 Tbsp, sour cream

Mix mayonnaise, cider vinegar, milk, sugar, and sour cream together in bowl, then toss into Cole slaw. Refrigerate for 2 hours.

CREAMY BROCCOLI & BACON SALAD

10oz container, cooking crème'
2 Tbsp, sugar
2 Tbsp, white vinegar
6 cups, small broccoli florets
6 slices, bacon, cooked and crumbled
1 small red onion, chopped
½ cup, shredded cheddar cheese
¼ cup, sunflower kernels

Mix first 3 ingredients in large bowl, add remaining ingredients; toss to coat. Refrigerate 1 hour.

FROSTY FRUIT SALAD

½ cup, sugar
½ tsp, white vinegar
1 egg, beaten
1 tsp, all-purpose flour
20 oz can of pineapple chunks
8oz container, whipped topping
1-1/2 cups, dry-roasted peanuts
1-1/2 cups, miniature marshmallows
2 cups, apples, peeled, de-cored, and chopped

Combine juice from pineapple, vinegar, sugar, egg, and flour in saucepan. Bring to a boil, stirring constantly. Cool. Fold in nondairy whipped topping. Combine apples, pineapple chunks, marshmallows, and peanuts. Blend in topping mixture.

PEPPERED CORN SALAD

2 cans, whole kernel corn, drained
1 medium, green pepper, chopped
1 medium, sweet red pepper, chopped
1 medium, onion, chopped
¼ cup, mayonnaise
¼ tsp, cayenne pepper
1 dash, garlic salt

In a bowl, combine all the ingredients. Cover and refrigerate for at least 2 hours.

SHAKE SALAD

1 head, romaine lettuce, washed and chopped
1 head, broccoli, washed and chopped
4 each, green onions, washed and chopped
1 package, ramen noodles, chopped
¼ cup, chopped nuts
½ cup, sugar
½ cup, canola oil
¼ cup, apple cider vinegar
1 Tbsp, soy sauce
2 dashes, salt
2 dashes, pepper

Toss together romaine lettuce, broccoli, green onions, ramen noodles, nuts, and set aside.

Mix sugar, oil, apple cider vinegar, soy sauce, salt, and pepper in bowl until well blended.

Place salad and sauce in large glass jar and shake until all is blended.

STRAWBERRY SALAD

1st Layer

3 cups, pretzels, crushed
½ cup, sugar
¾ cups, melted butter

Mix ingredients, place in bottom of 9x13 baking dish; bake 7-9 minutes at 400 degrees. Cool completely.

2nd Layer

8oz packet, cream cheese
12oz container, cool whip
½ cup, powdered sugar

Mix ingredients, and place over pretzel crust, chill until firm.

3rd Layer

6oz box, strawberry Jell-O
8oz can, crushed pineapple w/juice
12oz bag, frozen strawberries, cut in half
¼ cup, boiling water

Mix Jell-O and water, add pineapple with juice, and strawberries. Spread over 2nd layer and gel in refrigerator over night.

SUNSHINE SALAD

1 packet, lemon instant pudding
15oz can, Mandarin oranges, drained, juice set aside
15oz can, pineapple tidbits, drained, juice set aside
1 cup, Mandarin and pineapple juice
1 large package, strawberries
2 bananas, peeled and sliced at serving time

Mix lemon pudding with Mandarin and pineapple juice and set aside. Mix Mandarin oranges, pineapple tidbits, and strawberries in medium bowl, then add lemon pudding mixture and mix well. Refrigerate until set. Peel and slice bananas at serving time and place on top.

WALDORF SALAD

6 medium, apples, peeled and chopped
1 cup, walnut, chopped
1 cup, celery, chopped
¾ cup, grapes, sliced

Sauce

1-1/2 cup, mayonnaise
3 Tbsp, lemon juice
3 Tbsp, sugar
½ tsp, salt

Mix ingredients until blended in medium bowl, and set aside.

Salad mix

Toss together apples, walnuts, celery, and grapes in large bowl until blended. Add sauce mix and blend until all is coated. Refrigerate with covered lid for at least 2 hours.

SANDWICHES

BLUE MILL TAVERN LOOSEMEAT SANDWICH

1 lb, ground Beef
1 Tbsp, Crisco
2 Tbsp, salt
1 onion, medium, chopped fine
1 Tbsp, prepared yellow mustard
1 Tbsp, apple cider vinegar
1 Tbsp, sugar
Water to cover
Salt to taste
Pepper to taste

Take a cast iron skillet; melt Crisco over medium heat and lightly salt bottom of skillet. Break ground beef up in skillet, end being cooked up in small crumbles. Add chopped onion while browning meat. When meat is browned, add mustard, vinegar, sugar, and just enough water to barely cover meat in the pan. Cook at simmer until water is all cooked out, between 15 and 20 minutes. Adjust with salt and pepper to taste. Heat your hamburger buns; add yellow mustard and dill pickle slices on them. Serve with homemade potato salad or chips.

BOLOGNA SALAD

1 lb, bologna, ground with food processor
2 eggs, boiled and chopped
2 Tbsp, sweet relish
3 dollops, mayonnaise
Pepper to taste

Mix all ingredients in large bowl and serve on favorite sliced bread.

CALZONE CANADIAN-STYLE

1 tube, refrigerated pizza crust
½ cup, ricotta cheese
2oz, sliced Canadian bacon
1 cup, ham, cooked and diced
1 cup, mozzarella cheese, shredded

- Optional: Small amount of basil, parmesan cheese, and marinara sauce.

Unroll pizza crust, stretching into a 14x11 inch rectangle. Spread ricotta cheese on half of the dough lengthwise to within 1 inch of edge. Sprinkle Canadian bacon, ham and mozzarella cheese. Fold unfilled side of dough over filled half and press edges together. Transfer to greased baking sheet. Bake at 375 degrees for 30 minutes. Sprinkle with basil, and parmesan cheese, if desired. Slice; serve with marinara sauce for dipping.

ERIC'S STROMBOLI

1 can, refrigerated pizza crust
1 cup, pizza sauce
1 small package, sliced Canadian style bacon, sliced
1 small package, sliced pepperoni
1 cup, shredded mozzarella
¼ cup, onion, chopped
¼ Tbsp, Italian seasoning

Preheat oven to 375 degrees. Unroll dough; place on greased cookie sheet. Press dough into an 8x12 inch rectangle. Spread sauce on dough within 2 inches of the long edges and ½ inch on short sides. Top with remaining ingredients. Fold long sides of dough over filling; pinch all edges to seal. Bake for 25 minutes or until golden brown. Serve with pizza sauce.

FAMILY STYLE SLOPPY JOES

2 lbs, ground beef
1 large yellow onion, chopped
1-1/4 cup, ketchup or Catsup
½ cup, water
1 Tbsp, brown sugar
1 Tbsp, white vinegar
½ tsp, chili powder
Buns

Cook beef and onion over medium heat until meat is no longer pink; drain. Add ketchup or catsup, water, brown sugar, vinegar, salt and chili powder. Bring to a boil. Reduce heat and simmer uncovered for 30 minutes or longer. Serve over toasted buns.

GRILLED PIMENTO CHEESE SANDWICHES

1 cup, Miracle Whip
4oz jar, diced pimentos, drained
1 tsp, Worcestershire sauce
1 tsp, onion, finely grated
2, 8oz blocks, sharp cheddar cheese, shredded
Sliced bread, white, wheat, or sour dough

Stir together all ingredients, excluding Miracle Whip in medium bowl. Spread ¼ cup pimento cheese mixture on 1 side of sliced bread; top with another bread slice. Lightly spread both sides of sandwich with Miracle Whip. Repeat with remaining pimento cheese mixture for desired number of sandwiches. Cook, in batches, on a hot griddle or large nonstick skillet over medium heat 4 to 5 minutes on each side or until golden brown and cheese melts.

HAM SALAD

3 lbs, ham, ground with food processor
1 lb, ring bologna, ground with food processor
3 cups, sweet pickles, chopped
3 cups, salad dressing
1 cup, prepared yellow mustard
2oz jar, diced pimentos, drained

Mix all ingredients until well blended, place on sliced white, wheat, or sour dough bread.

LOOSEMEAT SANDWICHES

1 Tbsp, vegetable oil, 1 turn of pan
1-1/4 lbs, ground sirloin
1 cup, chicken stock, eyeball it, ½ a 14oz box
1 tsp, sweet paprika
¼ cup, Worcestershire sauce
¼ cup, apple cider vinegar
6oz can tomato paste
1/8 cup, ketchup or catsup
Salt to taste
Pepper to taste
4 hamburger buns, split, or Kaiser Rolls, split
½ yellow skinned onion, finely chopped

Heat a medium skillet over medium high heat. Add oil and meat to the pan and brown the meat, breaking it up with the back of a wooden spoon as it cooks. Add chicken stock to the meat. Season the meat with paprika, Worcestershire sauce, vinegar, tomato paste, ketchup or catsup, salt, and pepper. When the liquid comes to a bubble, reduce heat to simmer. Cook meat 15 minutes, stirring occasionally.

Pile meat into toasted buns or rolls and top with raw chopped onions.

PHILLY STEAK SLOPPY JO

1 lb, ground beef
1 sweet onion, chopped
1 green pepper, seeded and chopped
¼ cup, steak sauce
1 cup, beef broth
Provolone cheese
Hoagie buns

Crumble the ground beef into a skillet and add the chopped onion and green pepper. Begin to cook, when the beef is about half cooked, add the broth and steak sauce. Cook until items are done, allowing to simmer and cook down/thicken. Slice buns open and fill with meat mixture. Top with provolone cheese and place under broiler for 3 minutes.

QUESADILLA BURGER MELT

1 package, flour tortillas, medium
1 tomato, large, sliced
4 hamburgers, pre-cooked
1 packet, spicy dressing mix
2 Tbsp, butter, softened
¼ cup, red onion, diced
4 slices, bacon, cooked
16oz container, sour cream
Shredded pepper jack cheese
Shredded Mozzarella cheese

Heat a large skillet over medium heat. Combine spicy ranch mix with sour cream and set aside. For each burger, spread butter on one side of tortilla. Put tortilla in skillet, butter side down. Spread spicy ranch mix on tortilla and sprinkle evenly with both cheese leaving edges clean. Put some tomato, onion, and bacon over the cheese; add the burger to one side of the tortilla and fold over the shell. When the bottom side is browned, about 60 seconds, flip the quesadilla over and grill the other side.

SLOPPY JO MY WAY

1 lb, lean ground beef
¼ cup, onion, chopped
¼ cup, green bell pepper, chopped
½ tsp, garlic powder
1 tsp, prepared yellow mustard
¾ cup, ketchup
3 tsp, brown sugar
Salt to taste
Pepper to taste

In a medium skillet over medium heat, brown the ground beef, onion and green pepper; drain off liquids. Stir in the garlic powder, mustard, ketchup, and brown sugar; mix thoroughly. Reduce heat, and simmer to 30 minutes; season with salt and pepper.

VEGETABLE BEEF BARLEY SLOPPY JOES

1 lb, ground beef
1 can, vegetable beef barley soup
3 Tbsp, brown sugar
5 Tbsp, prepared yellow mustard
8 Tbsp, catsup
½ cup, apple cider vinegar
4 hamburger buns

Brown ground beef in large skillet. Add all ingredients, excluding hamburger buns, cook; turning ever couple of minutes until hot. Place on toasted hamburger buns.

SIDES

30-MINUTE SWEET CORNBREAD

1 box, jiffy yellow cake mix
1 box, jiffy cornbread mix
9x13 baking pan

Mix both boxes according to directions, and combine the batter. I generally use a large mixing bowl and add both boxes together. I add the other ingredients all at once. Spray baking pan with non-stick oil; bake at 350 degrees until done, about 30 minutes.

BACON

1 lb, bacon, sliced
1 large baking sheet
Foil to cover

Preheat oven to 375 degrees. Cover baking sheet with foil, and place sliced bacon evenly over baking sheet. Bake for 20 minutes.

BACON CHEDDAR PINWHEELS

8oz can, refrigerated crescent dinner rolls
½ cup, cheddar cheese, finely shredded
2 Tbsp, ranch dressing
¼ cup, green onions, chopped
¼ cup, bacon, cooked and crumbled

Preheat oven to 350 degrees. Unroll dough; separate into 2 long rectangles. Press each into a 12x4 inch rectangle, firmly pressing perforations to seal. Spread dressing over each rectangle to edges. Sprinkle each with bacon, cheese, and onions. Starting with one short side, roll up each rectangle; press edge to seal. With serrated knife, cut each roll into 8 slices; place on ungreased cookie sheet. Bake 12-17 minutes or until edges are deep golden brown. Immediately remove from cookie sheet, to serve warm.

BAKED MACARONI & CHEESE

16oz box, elbow macaroni
3 Tbsp, butter or margarine
1-1/2 cups, milk, divided
2 large eggs, lightly beaten
1 lb, Velveeta cheese, cubed in ½ inch sizes
2 cups, mild cheddar cheese, shredded and divided
2 cups, Monterrey jack cheese, shredded
1 tsp, salt
1 tsp, ground pepper

Set oven to 375 degrees. Cook macaroni in large pot of salted, boiling water until tender but not mushy, about 8-10 minutes. Drain well and pour into a large mixing bowl. Melt on low the Velveeta cheese and ¾ cup of milk until melted, stirring often. Pour melted cheese sauce over pasta and stir. Add in butter, ¾ cups milk, eggs, 1 cup shredded cheeses, salt and pepper. Mix well and transfer to a 2 quart baking dish. Pour the remaining cheese on top. Bake until top crust is golden brown and casserole is bubbling, about 25 minutes.

BROCCOLI CASSEROLE

1 package, frozen broccoli
2 cans, creamed corn
2 Tbsp, butter, melted
1 box, stuffing crumbs
2 eggs, beaten

Preheat oven to 350 degrees. Mix broccoli, corn, and eggs together. Mix stuffing and butter to spread over top.

Bake 1 hour.

EASY POTATOES

2 cans, sliced potatoes
1 cup, mayonnaise
1 cup, parmesan cheese
1 cup, shredded Colby/cheddar cheese

Place sliced potatoes in an 8x8 baking pan. Cover with mayonnaise. Cover with Parmesan cheese. Cover with shredded Colby/cheddar cheese. Bake at 325 degrees for 30 minutes.

FABULOUS & EASY POTATO CASSEROLE

2.5 lbs, hash browns
½ lb, shredded cheddar cheese
½ cup, onion, diced
1 cups, heavy whipping cream
1 Tbsp, salt
Pepper to taste

Preheat oven to 350 degrees, combine all ingredients; stir until well mixed. Butter or Pam spray large casserole dish. Place mixture into dish, cover and bake for 1 hour. Uncover, bake until golden brown. 20-25 minutes total baking time.

FRESH SKILLET BEANS

1 lb, green beans
1 cup, onion, chopped
2 garlic cloves, chopped
½ cup, red bell pepper, chopped
2 Tbsp, olive oil
1 cup, beef broth
½ tsp, salt
Pepper to taste

Snap the stems off the green beans. Melt olive oil in a skillet over medium low heat. Add garlic and onions and cook for 5 minutes, then add green beans and cook until they turn bright green. Add beef broth, chopped bell pepper, salt, and pepper. Turn heat to low and cover with lid, leaving lid cracked to allow for steam to escape. Cook for 45 minutes until liquid evaporates and beans are soft.

GARLIC CHEESE BISCUITS

2 cups, Bisquick mix
2/3 cups, milk
1 cup, shredded cheddar cheese
¼ stick, butter, melted
½ Tbsp, garlic powder

Set oven to 450 degrees. Mix Bisquick, milk, and shredded cheddar in large bowl. Drop large dollops of biscuit mixture onto large cookie sheet, and bake for 8-10 minutes.

Mix melted butter and garlic powder in bowl, and brush on top of hot biscuits when done. Serve warm.

GREEN BEAN CASSEROLE

2 cans, green beans
1 large onion, chopped and sauté in butter
2 Tbsp, flour
8oz container, sour cream
¼ cup, Velveeta cheese, cubed
1-1/2 cups, corn flakes
8 slices, American cheese

Preheat oven to 350 degrees. Grease 8x8 casserole dish. Mix green beans, onion, flour, sour cream, Velveeta cheese in large bowl and place into casserole dish. Top with sliced cheese, then corn flakes. Bake for 30 minutes or until brown.

MAC-N-CHEESE

1-1/4 lb, butter or margarine
2 Tbsp, all-purpose flour
1 lb, Velveeta cheese
1-1/2 cups, milk
2 cups, elbow macaroni, cooked as directed

Melt butter and add flour to blend. Cup up Velveeta into chunks, add to butter; stir to blend. Add milk, stir to blend and heat. Once smooth add to cooked noodles.

OVEN BAKED ASPARAGUS

1 lb, fresh asparagus, trimmed
2 Tbsp, butter
½ tsp, salt
Pepper to taste

Preheat oven to 350 degrees. Place asparagus on large piece of heavy-duty aluminum foil; dot with butter. Bring edges together and seal tightly; place on cookie sheet. Bake for 25-30 minutes. Shake with salt, and pepper to taste.

PLEASING CHEESY POTATOES

8 medium potatoes, washed
1 cup, butter, melted
1 Tbsp, vegetable oil
1-1/4 tsp, salt
¼ tsp, pepper
1 cup, cheddar cheese, grated

Slice each potato ¾ of the way through vertically. Roll potatoes in combination of oil and butter. Put potatoes in a shallow pan. Pour remaining butter over potatoes; season with salt and pepper. Bake at 375 degrees for 2 hours, basting with butter. Sprinkle cheese over potatoes and bake until cheese melts.

POTATO CASSEROLE

2 lbs, hash browns
1 cup, sour cream
1/3 cup, melted butter
1 can, cream of mushroom soup
1 can, cream of chicken soup
2 cups, shredded cheddar cheese
1 small onion, diced

Thaw hash browns; melt butter, and sauté onions. Add hash browns, melted butter, sautéed onions, soups, sour cream, and cheese. Mix all together in 13x9 inch glass casserole dish. Bake at 350 degrees for about 40 minutes, or until bubbling brown. Test that potatoes are soft.

SNAPPY ORANGES

6 medium oranges
2 medium grapefruit
1/8 tsp, baking soda
½ cup, sugar
¾ cup, honey
1/3 cup , white wine vinegar
1 stick of cinnamon
8 cloves, whole
1 dash, bottled hot pepper sauce
½ cup, raisins
1 cup, water

Peel fruit, reserving peel from 2 oranges. Remove white membrane from reserved peel; cut peel into thin strips. In saucepan, combine reserved peel, baking soda, and 1 cup water. Simmer covered, 10 minutes, and drain.

Remove membrane from fruits. Section oranges and grapefruit over a bowl; catching juices. Chop grapefruit. Discard seeds. In large saucepan, combine sugar, honey, vinegar, seasonings, and reserved peel. Bring to boiling: reduce heat. Simmer; uncovered. 10 minutes; remove. Add oranges, grapefruit, and raisins. Cool slightly. Place into jars, or moisture-vapor-proof containers. Refrigerate no more than 2 weeks.

Serve chilled with meats, poultry, or fish.

SQUASH CASSEROLE

4 cups, zucchini, diced
4 cups, yellow squash, diced
1 cup, yellow onion, chopped
1 box, Jiffy corn muffin mix (prepared as directed)
1 stick, butter
8oz, cheddar cheese, diced
3 cubes, chicken bouillon
1 tsp, garlic, minced
1 tsp, salt
½ tsp, ground pepper
½ tsp, thyme
1 Tbsp, parsley, chopped

Prepare Jiffy mix as directed, set aside to cool.

Place zucchini and yellow squash in a large saucepan and add just enough water to cover. Cook on medium low heat just until tender, remove from heat. Drain squash, reserve 1 cup of water for casserole. On medium low, place the butter in a large saucepan with onions and sauté until clear. Add salt, pepper, thyme, parsley, chicken bouillon cubes, garlic, and onions, stir. Add drained squash and diced cheese, stir. Crumble corn bread into squash mixture with reserved cup of water and mix well. Place squash mixture in 9x13 baking pan that has been sprayed with non-stick spray. Cover casserole and place in a preheated oven at 350 degrees. Bake for 60 minutes. Remove cover the last 20 minutes of baking time, to allow for browning.

ULTRA LOADED POTATOES

3 cups, chicken broth
5 large potatoes, diced
½ cup, cream
½ cup, sour cream
¼ cup, chives, chopped
2 Tbsp, butter
3 bacon slices, cooked and crumbled
2 dash, ground pepper

Heat broth and potatoes in large saucepan over medium high heat to a boil. Reduce heat to medium. Cover and cook 15 minutes, or until potatoes are tender. Drain reserving broth. Mash potatoes with ¼ cup broth, cream, sour cream, chives, butter, bacon and black pepper. Add additional broth if needed, until desired consistency. Garnish with remaining bacon.

SOUPS

10-MINUTE TAVERN CHILI

3 packets, McCormick's chili mix
3 lbs, ground beef
2 large cans, diced garlic/oregano tomatoes
3 cans, pinto beans
3 cans, red kidney beans
1 large yellow onion, diced

Brown ground beef in large skillet with diced yellow onion. When brown, place in large pot. Add McCormick's chili mix, diced tomatoes, pinto beans, and kidney beans with juices. Bring to a boil; simmer on low heat for 10 minutes.

Add cheese, chives, or your favorite topping for garnish.

AZTEC CHILI

2 lbs, ground beef
3 Tbsp, chili powder
2 tsp, sugar
1 large green pepper, diced
1 tsp, salt
15oz can tomato sauce
1 cup, water
2, 6oz cans, tomato paste
16oz can red kidney beans
8oz can whole kernel corn

Brown beef in large skillet drain off half of drippings. Sprinkle chili powder, sugar, and salt over meat. Stir in tomato sauce, water, and tomato paste, until blended. Add beans, corn, and green peppers. Cook over low heat for 1 hour, stirring occasionally.

Serve with grated cheese and corn chips.

BASIL TOMATO SOUP

2 large onions, chopped
4 Tbsp, olive oil, divided
3 large cans, Italian-style whole peeled tomatoes w/basil
1 box, chicken stock
1 cup, basil leaves
3 garlic cloves, chopped
1 tsp, lemon zest
1 Tbsp, lemon juice
1 tsp, salt
1 tsp, pepper
1 lb bag, frozen breaded okra

Sauté onions with 2 Tbsp oil in a large Dutch oven over medium high heat 9-10 minutes or until tender. Add tomatoes and chicken stock. Bring to a boil; reduce heat to medium low and simmer, stirring occasionally, about 30 minutes. Mix until smooth.

Mix basil, and next 4 ingredients with ¼ cup of water, and remaining 2 Tbsp of oil in a food processor until smooth. Stir basil mixture, sugar, and pepper into soup. Cook another 20 minutes or until heated thoroughly.

Cook okra according to package and serve with soup.

BROCCOLI CHEESE SOUP

¼ cup, margarine
¼ cup, onion, diced
2/3 cup, all-purpose flour
3, 10oz cans, chicken broth
¾ tsp, salt
1-1/4 cup, celery, chopped
1-1/4 cup, carrots, sliced
1 lb bag, frozen broccoli
1 lb box, Velveeta cheese, cubed
2 cups, whipping cream or half & half

Melt butter; add onion, flour and broth. Stir until smooth. Add rest of ingredients, cover and cook until heated thoroughly, stirring occasionally. Add cheese and half & half at the end, stirring until blended.

* Add extra cheese if you want to make yours especially cheesy.

CHEESE VEGETABLE SOUP

1 large onion, chopped
3 large potatoes, cubed
½ cup, celery, diced
½ cup, carrots, sliced or diced
2, 15oz cans, chicken broth
1 lb bag, frozen broccoli & cauliflower
2 cans, cream of chicken soup
1 lb box, Velveeta cheese, cubed
¼ cup, beer (optional)
½ tsp, Cajun seasonings (optional)
½ tsp, Tabasco sauce (optional)

Place all vegetables in large pot and cook in broth until tender; about 20-30 minutes. Add cream of chicken soup, beer, seasonings, and Velveeta cheese. Cook until smooth and creamy.

CHICKEN NOODLE SOUP

2 large cans, chunked chicken breast, drained
1 lb bag, Kluski noodles
1 can, carrots, sliced
1 small onion, diced
1 large can, cream of chicken soup
5 cups, chicken stock
2 cups, chicken broth
2 cups, celery, chopped
2 tsp, chicken bouillon powder
2 tsp, garlic powder
1 tsp, garlic salt
1 tsp, Lawry's season salt
½ tsp, pepper
½ stick, butter

Cook Kluski noodles for 10 minutes; drain, do not rinse.
Caramelize; celery and onions with butter. Add all ingredients to
a large stock pot; heat to boiling. Reduce heat; simmer on low
heat for 2 hours.

CREAMY POTATO AND ONION SOUP

2 Tbsp, butter
1 Tbsp, olive oil
4 large sweet onions, chopped
1 tsp, sugar
3 Tbsp, all-purpose flour
32oz box, chicken broth
32oz bag, frozen southern-style cubed hash browns
½ tsp, dried thyme
1 each, bay leaf
1 tsp, salt
½ tsp, pepper
1 cup, grated Swiss cheese
1 cup, half and half

Garnish: chopped chives, and ground pepper

Melt butter with oil in a large Dutch oven over medium heat. Add onions and sugar. Cook, stirring often, 45-60 minutes or until onions become caramel colored. Sprinkle onions with flour, and stir to coat. Add chicken broth. Bring to a boil over medium heat, and cook 20 minutes. Add hash browns and 2 cups water. Reduce heat to low, add thyme and next 3 ingredients; simmer 30 minutes. Stir in cheese and half-and-half; cook, stirring constantly, over medium heat 5 minutes or until cheese is melted. Remove bay leaf before serving. Garnish, if desired.

CREAMY CHICKEN DIVAN SOUP

2 Tbsp, butter
1 medium sweet onion, chopped
1 garlic clove, chopped
¼ tsp, dried crushed red pepper
48oz can, chicken broth
2, 12oz bags, broccoli florets
8oz package, cream cheese, cubed
4 cups, chicken, cooked and chopped
8oz block, sharp cheddar cheese, shredded
2 tsp, salt
1 tsp, pepper

Garnish: toasted slivered almonds

Melt butter in Dutch oven over medium high heat; adding onion, and sauté 5 minutes or until tender. Add garlic and red pepper, and cook 2 minutes. Stir in chicken broth and broccoli. Cover and bring to a boil; reduce heat to medium, and cook 15 minutes or until broccoli is tender. Stir in cream cheese. Stir mixture with handheld blender until smooth. Add chicken and shredded cheese. Cook, stirring occasionally; about 5 minutes or until cheese is melted. Add salt and pepper to season. Serve immediately with almonds, if desired.

CREAMY CHICKEN NOODLE SOUP

2 Tbsp, butter
2 cups, carrots, chopped
1 cup, celery, chopped
1 cup, onion, chopped
2 each, chicken breast
6 cups, chicken broth
1 cup, milk
2 cans, cream of chicken soup
1 lb bag, Kluski egg noodles

Melt butter in a large sauce pan. Saute' veggies in butter. Add chicken broth, and bring to a boil. Add chicken breasts, boiling until cooked through; about 10 minutes. Remove chicken breast, set aside to be shredded. Add milk; bring to a boil. Add shredded chicken, and noodles; cook until noodles are done, about 15 minutes. Add cream of chicken soup and simmer for 15 minutes.

EASY POTATO SOUP

1 lb, sausage
1 medium onion, diced
2 box, chicken broth
1 lb, potatoes, diced
1 can, cream of celery soup
1 can of heavy cream

Brown sausage with onion, and add to large pot. Add chicken broth and potatoes; boiling until potatoes are cooked and tender. Add celery soup and heavy cream; stirring until heated thoroughly.

ERIC'S BEEF VEGETABLE NOODLE SOUP

1 lb bag, Kluski noodles
2 lbs, ground beef
2 bags, frozen soup vegetables
46oz can, tomato Juice
2 cans, beef consommé
1 box, beef broth
Salt to taste

Cook Kluski noodles for 10 minutes, draining without rinsing. Fry ground beef. Combine all ingredients to a large pot; cooking for 1 hour on medium heat; salt to taste. Serve with garlic toast or saltines.

ERIC'S CHILI RECIPE

2 lbs, ground beef
2 lbs, sausage, mild
1 large onion, diced
1 garlic clove, diced
2 cans, red kidney beans, with juice
2 cans, pinto beans, with juice
2 cans, navy beans, with juice
1 large can, tomato sauce
1 packet, 2 alarm chili fixings
1 small jalapeno, seeds removed and diced

Garnish: cheddar cheese, cubed and crackers

Brown ground beef and sausage in large skillet with onion, garlic, 2 alarm chili fixings, and jalapeno. Add meat mixture to large pot. Add red kidney beans with juice, pinto beans with juice, navy beans with juice, and tomato sauce. Stir to blend. Cook on low heat for 5 hours. Serve with cheese and crackers.

ERIC'S VEGETABLE BEEF SOUP

46oz can tomato juice
2 lbs, ground beef
2 bags, frozen soup vegetables
1 bag, Kluski noodles
1 box, Lipton onion soup mix
2 cans, beef consommé
1 cup, beef broth

Cook ground beef, combine all ingredients, excluding noodles in large pot. Cook for 1 hour. Prepare Kluski noodles per instructions; add to pot, mixing well. Continue cooking for 30 minutes.

ERIK'S BAKED POTATO SOUP

5 large baking potatoes, washed
6 cups, milk
2/3 cup, butter
2/3 cup, all-purpose flour
1 cup, sour cream
2 cups, real bacon pieces
1 cup, shredded cheddar cheese
Olive oil
Salt
Pepper

Preheat oven to 425 degrees. Rub baking potatoes with olive oil, shake with salt and pepper to coat; pricking potatoes with fork. Place on baking sheet; cooking for 1 hour. Remove potato peel, if desired, break up potatoes with fork; placing in large pot. Add all other ingredients; cooking on top of stove with low heat for 30 minutes, or until heated thoroughly.

ERIK'S CHICKEN SOUP

1 whole chicken, washed
1 whole onion, chopped
9 cubes, chicken bouillon cubes
4 medium carrots, sliced
1 Tbsp, parsley flakes
1 garlic clove, chopped
2 tsp, salt
1 tsp, pepper
1 bag, Kluski noodles

In large kettle, place whole chicken, removing the giblets. Add onion, garlic, and enough water to barely cover the chicken. Bring to a boil. Reduce heat to medium, cover and simmer to low boil for about 1 hour or until chicken pulls off bone easily. Remove chicken. Strain broth and reserve. Cool chicken slightly and remove from bone; chopping in larger pieces. Return chicken to broth, add carrots and seasonings. Boil on medium 45 minutes or until carrots are tender. Add noodles and cook 15 minutes or until tender. Mix well, and serve.

ERIK'S CHICKEN & NOODLES

1 bag, Oakland noodles
1 whole rotisserie chicken, cooked and shredded
1 can, cream of chicken soup
2 boxes, chicken broth
1 can, large buttery biscuits
Butter to taste

Cook Oakland noodles per instructions, utilizing chicken broth in place of water, do not drain. Add rotisserie chicken, and cream of chicken soup. Heat to boiling, and remove from heat. Cook biscuits per instructions. Serve chicken & noodles over buttered biscuits.

ERIK'S QUICK POTATO SPINACH SOUP

1 lb, mild sausage
64oz can, chicken broth
2 cans, diced potatoes
1 can, cream of celery soup
1 cup, heavy cream
1 can, spinach

Cook sausage in skillet, do not drain. Add sausage and all ingredients to large pot; bringing to a boil. Simmer on low for 1 hour.

HOMEGROWN CHILI

4 lbs, ground beef
1 can, tomato sauce
1 large can, tomato juice
1 can, chicken broth
1 can, beef broth
1 can, beer
3 cans, pinto beans w/juice
8 Hungarian wax peppers, diced
2 cayenne peppers, diced
8 jalapeno peppers, diced
2 medium green peppers, diced
2 large onions, diced
10 garlic cloves, minced
2 tsp, ground oregano
8 Tbsp, chili powder
4 Tbsp, ground cumin
2 tsp, salt
1 tsp, sugar

Brown beef in large skillet with all raw vegetables; do not drain. Place into large stock pot with all other ingredients. Bring to a boil, reduce to simmer; cooking for 2 hours.

PRESSURE COOKER CHILI

1.5 lbs, pork butt roast, cut in small pieces
2, 7.5oz cans, green chili salsa
2, 10oz cans, tomatoes & green chilies
1 tsp, green chili peppers, diced
1 large onion, diced
1 tsp, salt
½ tsp, chili powder
1 pinch, cumin
1.5 cups, water

Pressure cook roast until tender; remove excess water and fat. Add salsa, tomatoes & green chilies, chili peppers, onion, salt, chili powder, and 1.5 cups of water. Run pressure up and cook for 30 minutes. Add pinch of cumin before serving.

SKILLET CHILI

1.5 lbs, ground beef, cooked and drained
1 pinch, garlic salt
2 medium green peppers, diced
1 large onion, diced
2, 16oz cans, red kidney beans, drained
16oz can, tomato sauce
2, 16oz cans, Italian stewed tomatoes
1 dash, cayenne pepper
1 tsp, garlic salt
1 tsp, chili powder

Cook in skillet on top of stove for 1 hour at low to medium heat.

SOMETHING LIKE WENDY'S CHILI

2 lbs, ground beef, cooked and drained
29oz can, tomato sauce
29oz can, kidney beans w/liquid
29oz can, pinto beans w/liquid
1 cup, onion, diced
2, 15oz cans, tomatoes, diced
2 tsp, cumin powder
3 tsp, chili powder
1 cup, water
2 tsp, salt
1 tsp, pepper

Cook ground beef with onions in large skillet. Transfer into large pot; adding all other ingredients. Bring to a boil; reducing heat, and simmering for 2 hours.

TACO SOUP

1.5 lbs, ground beef, extra lean
1 medium onion, diced
15oz can, great northern beans w/liquid
15oz can, pinto beans w/liquid
15oz can, red kidney beans w/liquid
15oz can, black beans w/liquid
1 packet, McCormick's taco seasoning
1 packet, ranch dressing mix
28oz can, tomatoes, diced
1 cup, water

Brown and drain the beef and onions. Toss it and everything else in the slow cooker on low heat and let it cook all day. It can be done on the stove at a higher heat, but it's much better in the crock pot. If adventurous, add 1 can of Mexican corn & chili beans. Serve with grated cheese of your choice.

VEGETABLE SOUP, ROAST STYLE

1 small cheap roast of any kind
¼ cup, all-purpose flour
1 cup, water
3 medium potatoes, diced
1 bag, frozen mixed vegetables
64oz can, tomato juice

Cut roast into chunks, flour and brown in skillet w/olive oil. Place in Dutch oven, adding a cup of water to meat drippings. Stir to blend. Add potatoes, frozen mixed vegetables, and tomato juice; stirring well to blend. Simmer on low heat for 3 hours.

WHITE BEAN COLLARD SOUP

2 slices bacon, hickory smoked
2 cups, smoked ham, chopped
1 medium onion, diced
5, 16oz cans, navy beans
1 cup, cattlemen's barbecue sauce
6oz can, tomato paste
1 Tbsp, chicken bouillon granules
1 tsp, ground chipotle Chile pepper
½ tsp, dried thyme
½ tsp, ground pepper
3 cups, shredded collard greens
8 cups, water

Garnish: hot sauce

Cook bacon in a large Dutch oven over medium-high heat, 5 minutes or until crisp; remove bacon, and drain on paper towel. Reserve 2 tablespoons of drippings in Dutch oven. Crumble bacon. Saute' ham and onion in hot drippings 15 minutes or until tender. Add beans, and rest of ingredients, excluding collard greens. Bring to a boil over medium-high heat. Cover; reduce heat to medium-low, and simmer, stirring occasionally, 1 hour. Stir in collards; cook 15 minutes or until tender. Serve with crumbled bacon and hot sauce.

WHITE CHILI

2 tsp, olive oil
2 medium onions, chopped
4 garlic cloves, minced
4 skinless chicken breasts, cooked & chopped
3, 15oz cans, chicken broth or stock
8oz can, green chilies, chopped
2 tsp, cumin
2 tsp, dried oregano
½ tsp, cayenne pepper
5, 14oz cans, great northern beans w/liquid
1 cup, shredded Monterey jack cheese

Simmer oil in large pot. Saute' onions and garlic for 10 minutes.
Add chicken, broth, green chilies, cumin, oregano, and pepper;
bringing to a boil.

Reduce heat, add beans. Simmer for 45 minutes. Pour into
individual bowls and top with cheese and cilantro.

ZESTY TOMATO SOUP

1 packet, zesty Italian dry mix
3 cans, tomato soup
3 cans, water from tomato soup
1 package, pepperoni, chopped

Garnish: mozzarella cheese, grated and croutons

Add all ingredients to medium pot, excluding garnishes. Mix well, cooking on low heat for 1 hour. Serve in individual bowls, garnished with mozzarella cheese and croutons.

CROCK-POT

BACON CHEESEBURGER CREME SOUP

1 lb, ground beef
8oz stick, Velveeta cheese, cubed
1 bag, Ore-Ida hash browns
3 bags, bacon bits
32oz box, chicken broth or stock
1 can, French's fried onions
1 small onion, diced (optional)
1 container, Philadelphia cooking crème, original flavor

Brown ground beef and add to crock-pot. Add all other ingredients to the pot, excluding French's fried onions. Cook on low for 4-5 hours.

Top with French's fried onions and ENJOY!

BACON CHEESEBURGER SOUP

1 lb, ground beef
2 lbs, Velveeta cheese, cubed
2 lbs, hash browns
2 small bags, bacon bits
30oz box, chicken stock

Brown ground beef and add to crock-pot. Then add all other ingredients to pot, cook on low for 4-5 hours.

BARBECUE PORK

1, 4 lb Boston butt pork shoulder roast, trimmed
18oz bottle, cattlemen's barbecue sauce
12oz bottle, coca-Cola

Place roast in a lightly greased 6-qt. slow cooker; pour barbecue sauce and cola over roast. Cover and cook on low 10 hours or until meat shreds easily with a fork.

Transfer pork to a cutting board; shred with two forks, leaving in fat for flavor. Return to slow cooker, and mix with barbecue sauce.

Serve with your favorite buns, or hoagies.

BEEF & NOODLES

1.5 lbs, beef tips
1 can, cream of mushroom soup
1 can, beef broth
1 packet, onion soup mix
1 package, egg noodles

Place beef tips into crock-pot, pouring beef broth over top. Mix cream of mushroom soup with onion soup mix and pour into pot. Cook on low for 8 hours.

Prepare egg noodles per package instructions; serving beef tips over egg noodles.

BEER ITALIAN VEEF

1 large rump roast
2 packets, dry Italian dressing
1 can of your favorite beer
1 jar, cherry or Pepperoncini peppers w/juice

Place roast into crock-pot; shaking dry Italian dressing over top of roast. Pour in beer; adding peppers. Cover and cook on low for 10 hours.

Serve with favorite hoagie buns.

CHICKEN & NOODLES

20oz bag, wide egg noodles
1 stick, butter
1 can, cream of mushroom soup
1 packet, ranch dressing
1 packet, Italian dressing
2 cans, cream of chicken soup
1 box, chicken broth
1 box, chicken stock
3 large cans, dark & white meat chicken

Place butter, mushroom & chicken soup, ranch & Italian dressing, chicken broth & stock, and cans of chicken into crock-pot. Cook on high for 3 hours. Add egg noodles & cook for 30 minutes, stirring 2 to 3 times. Add pepper to taste, and ENJOY!

Serve over toasted bread or mashed potatoes.

CHICKEN or BEEF ENCHILADA CASSEROLE

4 boneless; skinless raw chicken breast
2 lbs, ground beef, cooked (for beef enchilada)
28oz can, red enchilada sauce
11.7oz bag, corn tortillas
3 cups, shredded cheddar cheese, divided
2, 3.8oz cans, Black olives
16oz container, sour cream for garnish
1 small bottle, chives for garnish

Place chicken breast into crock-pot and add red enchilada sauce. Cook on high 4 hours. Shred with 2 forks. Cut corn tortillas into strips and place into crock-pot, and stir. Place 1.5 cups of shredded cheddar into crock-pot, and stir. Place 1 can of black olives into crock-pot, and stir. Flatten out with spatula. Spread other can of black olives over top of chicken, spreading other 1.5 cups of shredded cheddar over top. Cook on high for 1 hour. Place on plates with dollop of sour cream and chives.

* If wanting beef instead of chicken, follow recipe with cooked ground beef.

CHILI

2 lbs, ground beef, cooked and drained
16oz can, mild chili beans
2, 16oz cans, red kidney beans
2, 16oz cans, mushrooms
10oz can, tomato paste
10oz can, tomato sauce
2 medium onions, diced
2 medium jalapenos, diced
2 medium green peppers, diced
2 dashes, garlic powder
2 dashes, onion powder
2 dashes, chili powder
1 large can, Brooks mild chili beans

Brown ground beef, draining grease. Add finely chopped onions, green peppers, and jalapenos. Stir. Add beans, tomato sauce, and tomato paste. Stir. Add garlic powder, onion powder, and chili powder to taste. Stir in drained mushrooms. Slow cook for 4 hours.

CRAZY CHICKEN CRACK SOUP

4 large cans, chicken, w/dark and white meat
8oz, spaghetti noodles, uncooked
1 cup, shredded Mozzarella
6 slices bacon, cooked and crumbled
1 small yellow onion, diced
2 large carrot, diced
2 stalks, celery, diced
2 Tbsp, olive oil
32oz box, chicken stock
10.75oz can, cream of chicken soup
1 cup, half and half
1 packet, dry Italian seasoning
4 dashes, salt
4 dashes, pepper

Heat olive oil in a large stock pot over medium-high heat and saute' onion, carrot and celery until softened; season with salt and pepper. Add dry Italian mix and cook for 3 minutes, stirring until veggies are evenly coated. Add chicken stock and chicken soup; stirring together. Mix in spaghetti, bacon and chicken; bringing to a boil. Reduce heat to low and cook for 30. Stir in Mozzarella cheese and half-and-half. Cook another 10 minutes.

Serve with favorite mashed potatoes.

CREAMY ITALIAN CHICKEN

4 boneless, chicken breast halves
1 envelope, Italian salad dressing mix
¼ cup, water
8oz package, cream cheese, softened
1 can, cream of chicken soup, undiluted
4oz can, mushroom stems and pieces, drained
1 lb bag, cooked rice or noodles

Place chicken in crock-pot. Combine the salad dressing mix and water; pour over chicken. Cover and cook on low for 3 hours. In a small mixing bowl, beat cream cheese and soup until blended. Stir in mushrooms. Pour over chicken; cooking 1 hour.

Serve over rice or noodles.

CROCK-POT STRING POTATOES

32 oz bag, hash browns
1 can, cream of mushroom soup
½ cup, margarine
1 can, cheddar cheese soup
1 cup, sour cream
½ cup, bacon bits

Put hash browns in small crock pot. Mix soups and sour cream together. Pour over hash browns. Cut up margarine and stir into hash browns. Top w/bacon bits, and cook on low for 5 hours, stirring occasionally.

CROCK POT PIZZA

2 lbs, ground beef
1 can, hunts spaghetti sauce (your favorite)
1 bottle, Contadina pizza sauce
1 package, Kluski noodles
2 packages, pepperoni slices
4 packages, Mexican shredded 4-cheese

Brown ground beef, add spaghetti and pizza sauce; simmering 10 minutes. Cook Kluski noodles for 10 minutes. Place a layer of beef mixture into bottom of crock pot, then layer of Kluski noodles, a layer of pepperoni slices, then layer of Mexican shredded 4-cheese. Do a second layer. Cook in crock pot on low for 2 hours.

* Black olives can be added for a little extra flavor.

CUBED STEAK W/GRAVY

2 packets, au jus gravy mix
1 can, cream of chicken soup
1 can, French onion soup
½ cup, water
2 lbs, cube steak
3 Tbsp, cornstarch
3 Tbsp, cold water

In the bottom of a 6-quart slow cooker, combine cream of chicken soup; French onion soup, packet of au jus and ½ cup of water. Stir well. Put cubed steak in slow cooker w/gravy mixture. Cover slow cooker and cook steak on low for 10 hours. After cooking; thicken gravy. In a small bowl, whisk together cornstarch and cold water. Stir mixture into crock pot. Turn the setting to high and cook for 45 minutes, or until gravy has thickened.

* Serve with mashed potatoes.

ENCHILADA CASSEROLE

2 lbs, ground beef
1 whole onion, diced
3 cans, enchilada sauce
½ package, corn tortillas, cut into triangles
2 cups, shredded cheddar, divided
1 small can, black olives
1 container, sour cream for garnish

Brown ground beef w/onions and place into crock pot. Add 3 cans enchilada sauce, and stir until blended. Add corn tortillas; mixing well. Add shredded cheddar, and black olives to top. Cook on high for 1 hour.

* Garnish w/sour cream and serve.

ERIC'S BEEF STEW

2 lbs, ground beef, cooked; not drained
1 tsp, Worcestershire sauce
1 large onion, chopped
1.5 cups, beef broth
½ tsp, salt
½ tsp, pepper
1 garlic clove, diced
3 medium potatoes, diced
4 carrots, diced
1 can, green beans
1 can, whole corn
1 bay leaf
2 packets, McCormick's brown gravy mix
¼ cup, all-purpose flow
1 cup, fresh sliced mushrooms
1 packet, dry onion soup mix
1 can, golden mushroom soup

Place all in large crock pot on low for 12-hours, or on high for 6 hours.

ERIC'S CHICKEN AND DUMPLINGS

2, 1 lb bags, Colavita Gnocchi of potato
2, 15.25oz cans, chunky classic chicken noodle soup
2, 12.5oz cans, chunk chicken breast w/juices
2, 10.5oz cans, cream of chicken soup
1, 10.5oz can, cream of mushroom soup
2 quarts, water

Bring water to a boil on stove. Add Colavita gnocchi of potato, cooking for 4 minutes. Gnocchi will float to the surface when done. Add to crock-pot. Mix all other ingredients to the pot, stirring well. Cook on low for 2 hours, or high for 1 hour.

Serve w/biscuits.

ERIC'S ITALIAN BEEF

1, 5lb rump roast
1 packet, Italian dressing mix
1 cup, water
1 packet, au jus gravy mix
2 tsp, Italian seasoning
6 Pepperoncini peppers

Mix together water, gravy mix, dressing and Italian seasoning. Pour over roast in crock-pot. Add peppers, if desired; cooking on low for 4 hours. Break up roast and cook 2 more hours.

Serve with favorite hoagie buns.

ERIC'S LASAGNA

2 lbs, ground beef
16oz package, turkey sausage
1 jar, Home-style Ragu thick spaghetti sauce
1 bottle, Contadina pizza sauce
2 small boxes, Cremette oven ready lasagna noodles
16oz container, large curd cottage cheese
16oz container, fresh parmesan cheese
2, 16oz packages, shredded mozzarella cheese

Brown ground beef, and turkey in large skillet; adding spaghetti and pizza sauce, heating to bubbling. Place half meat sauce in bottom of crock-pot; add 3 layers of oven ready lasagna noodles, breaking in pieces to fit. Add ½ container of cottage cheese, ½ container of parmesan cheese, and 1 package of mozzarella cheese. Repeat another layer. Cook in crock-pot on low for 4 hours. Turn off and let stand for 30 minutes.

ERIK'S BEEF POT ROAST

3 lb chuck roast, nicely marbled
1 packet, ranch dressing mix
1 packet, zesty Italian dressing mix
1 packet, McCormick's brown gravy mix
½ cup water
1 whole, white sweet onion, in rounds
1 can, sliced carrots, drained
1 can, sliced potatoes, drained

Place chuck roast in bottom of crock-pot. Mix ranch dressing, zesty Italian dressing; McCormick's brown gravy mix with ½ cup water and pour over chuck roast. Place onion, carrots, and potatoes over the top. Cook on high for 2 hours, low for 4 hours.

* Best served with fresh cornbread.

ERIK'S ITALIAN BEEF

1, 3lb chuck roast, well marbled
1 packet, Italian dressing mix
¼ bottle, Pepperoncini peppers
½ bottle, Italian dressing

Place roast in bottom of crock-pot. Shake Italian dressing mix over roast, adding Pepperoncini peppers, pouring Italian dressing over top.

Cook on low for 8-10 hours. Serve with favorite hoagie buns.

ERIK'S LASAGNA

2 lbs, ground beef
32oz jar, Classico spaghetti sauce
2 cups, small curd cottage cheese
4 cups, shredded mozzarella cheese
1 box, ready to cook lasagna noodles, uncooked
2 packages, shredded mixed cheese to cover

Brown ground beef, adding Classico spaghetti sauce;
simmering until hot. Mix cottage cheese and mozzarella
cheese in separate bowl. Place portion of meat sauce in
bottom of crock-pot, add layer of lasagna noodles, and layer
of cottage cheese/mozzarella mixture. Repeat as above x 1.
Add shredded mix blend cheese to cover top.

Cook in crock-pot on low for 4 hours.

FARMER'S BREAKFAST

32oz package, frozen hash browns
1 package, mild sausage crumbles
2 cups, shredded mozzarella cheese
½ cup, shredded parmesan cheese
½ cup, julienne cut sun dried tomatoes, packed in oil, drained
6 green onions, sliced
12 eggs
½ cup, milk
½ tsp, salt
¼ tsp, ground black pepper

Spray a 6 quart slow cooker with cooking spray. Place ½ of potatoes on bottom of slow cooker. Top with half of the sausage, mozzarella and parmesan cheese, sun dried and green onion. Repeat layering. Beat eggs, milk, salt and pepper in large bowl with wire whisk until well blended. Pour evenly over potato-sausage mixture. Cook on low setting for 8 hours or on high setting for 4 hours, or until eggs are done.

FRENCH ONION SOUP

2 quarts, beef stock
6 cups, yellow onion, sliced
1/2 cup, sugar
1/2 cup, butter
2 cup, parmesan cheese
2 tsp, salt
4 tsp, flour

Pour beef stock in crock-pot; cover and set on high. Cook onions slowly in large skillet w/butter; cooking covered for 10 minutes. Add salt, sugar, and flour; stirring well. Add to stock in crock pot. Cover and cook on low for 8 hours or on high for 4. Garnish w/Parmesan cheese.

ITALIAN CHICKEN

4 each, large chicken breast
1 packet, zesty Italian dressing
8oz package, cream cheese, softened
2 cans, cream of chicken soup

Place chicken breast in bottom of crock pot. Mix zesty Italian dressing, cream cheese, and cream of chicken soup together in bowl, then place over chicken breast.

Cook on low for 4 hours.

- Serve on top of pasta noodles

ITALY'S HOME-STYLE POT ROAST

8oz can, sliced mushrooms, sliced
1 large, sweet onion, sliced
1, 4 lb, boneless chuck roast, fat left on
1 tsp, black pepper
2 Tbsp, Olive oil
1 packet, dry onion soup mix
14oz can, beef stock
8oz, tomato sauce
3 Tbsp, tomato paste
2 tsp, dried Italian dressing
2 Tbsp, cornstarch

Place mushrooms and onion in a lightly greased 6 quart slow cooker. Sprinkle roast with pepper. Cook roast in hot oil in a large skillet over medium-high heat 5 minutes on each side, or until browned. Place roast on top of mushrooms and onion in slow cooker. Sprinkle onion soup mix over roast; pour beef stock and tomato sauce over roast. Cover and cook on low for 10 hours.

Transfer roast to a cutting board; cutting into large chunks. Keep roast warm.

Stir tomato paste and Italian seasoning into slow cooker. Stir together cornstarch and 2 Tbsp of water in a small bowl until smooth; adding to juices in slow cooker, stirring until blended. Increase slow cooker heat to high. Cover and cook 1 hour. Return roast to crock-pot; mixing well, cooking another 30 minutes.

* Serves well with cornbread.

KRAZY CHICKEN TORTILLA

4 cups, chopped, cooked chicken
1 large onion, chopped
1 large green bell pepper, chopped
10.75oz can, cream of chicken soup
10.75oz can, cream of mushroom soup
10oz can, diced tomatoes w/green Chiles
1 garlic clove, minced
1 tsp, chili powder
12, 6 inch corn tortillas
2 cups, shredded sharp cheddar cheese

Stir together first 8 ingredients. Tear tortillas into 1 inch pieces; layer 1/3 of tortilla pieces in a lightly greased 6 quart slow cooker. Top with 1/3 of chicken mixture and 2/3 cup cheese. Repeat layers 2 times.

Cover and cook on low for 4 hours, or until golden brown.

LITTLE E'S BEEF SOUP

2 lbs, ground beef
½ bottle, Clamato juice
10 cubes, beef bouillon
28oz can tomato sauce
2, 14.5oz cans, diced tomatoes w/green pepper & onion
14.5oz can whole kernel corn
14.5oz can diced potatoes
14.5oz can carrots
14.5oz can, Margaret Holmes seasoned pepper n' peas
14.5oz can green beans
Italian seasoning
Lawry's season salt

While browning ground beef, empty all cans w/juice into crock pot. Add Clamato juice and beef bouillon cubes. Set crock pot to 10 hour low. Place cooked hamburger, un-drained, into crock pot. Shake to taste, Lawry's season salt, and Italian seasoning sake.

* Wonderful with homemade cheese biscuits.

MCCORMICK CHICKEN

4 large chicken thighs
2 large chicken legs
2 large chicken breasts
1 can, whole tomatoes
McCormick's Montreal chicken rub
Extra virgin olive oil

Place chicken pieces in bottom of crock-pot, drizzle extra virgin olive oil over top of chicken, shake with McCormick's Montreal chicken rub generously over the top. Put 6 whole tomatoes in crock-pot without the juice. Turn crock-pot to high for 2 hours, low for 4.

MEATBALLS & NOODLES

20oz bag, wide egg noodles
1 stick, butter
1 can, cream of mushroom soup
1 bag, Home-style meatballs, 20 meatballs
2 cans, golden mushroom soup
1 box, beef broth
1 box, beef stock

Place stick of butter, cream of mushroom, golden mushroom, meatballs, and broth into crock-pot. Cook on high for 2 hours. Add egg noodles, cook for 45 minutes, stirring 5 times. Add salt and pepper.

MEATLOAF O'MINE

2 lbs, ground beef
1 packet, dry onion soup mix
1 cup, shredded sharp cheddar cheese
¾ cup, dry breadcrumbs
1 large, egg
1 Tbsp, Worcestershire sauce
1 cup, ketchup, divided
1 Tbsp, brown sugar
1 tsp, prepared yellow mustard

Combine first 6 ingredients, ½ cup ketchup, and ¼ cup water; shape mixture into a loaf. Line bottom and sides of crock-pot with aluminum foil, allowing 2 inches to extend over sides. Lightly grease foil. Place loaf in slow cooker.

Stir together brown sugar, mustard, and remaining ½ cup ketchup; spread over top of meatloaf. Cover and cook on low for 6 hours or until a meat thermometer comes out at 160 degrees. Lift loaf from slow cooker, using foil sides as handles. Let stand 15 minutes before serving.

MEXICAN FARMER'S CASSEROLE

2 lbs, ground beef
1 medium, onion, chopped
2 Tbsp, butter
3.25 cups, taco seasoning
1 cup, water
6oz can tomato paste
1 cup, v8 juice
1 large bottle, taco sauce
1 can, whole kernel corn, drained
1 can, diced potatoes,
½ package, corn tortillas, chopped, and divided
4 medium, tomatoes, chopped
4 cups, shredded cheddar cheese, divided

Brown ground beef in large fry pan. Saute' onions w/butter in small sauce pan. Add onions to ground beef. Add taco seasoning and water to ground beef mixture. Simmer for 15 minutes.

In medium sauce pan, add tomato paste, v8 juice, taco sauce, corn, potatoes, and tomatoes; heating until warm.

Place ½ meat mixture to bottom of crock-pot, then ½ of sauce mixture, then ½ corn tortillas, then ½ of shredded cheese. Repeat layers. Cook on high for 2 hours; low for 1 hour.

Serve w/dollops of sour cream, and taco sauce to taste. Garnish w/cilantro.

MUSHROOM ITALIAN BEEF

3 lb chuck roast, well marbled
3 packets, dry Italian seasoning mix
1 small can, sliced mushrooms w/juice
½ bottle, banana peppers w/juice

Place roast in large crock-pot. Shake dry Italian seasoning mix over roast. Add mushrooms and banana peppers.

Cook on low for 10-12 hours.

* Serve with favorite hoagie buns.

SHELLY'S BEEF STEW

2 lbs, beef stew meat, roll in flow and brown
1 bag, baby red potatoes
1 onion, chopped
1 bag, baby carrots
2 cans, original Ro-Tel tomatoes
2 cans, mild Ro-Tel tomatoes
3 cans, Italian style green beans
1 can, Manwich sauce (not-so-Sloppy Jo sauce w/be thicker)
2 boxes, beef stock
Salt to taste
Pepper to taste

Add all ingredients to extra large crock-pot, and cook on low for 6 hours.

SPICY STEAK & BLACK BEEN CHILI

2 lbs, sirloin steak, cubed
2 Tbsp, vegetable oil
3, 15.5oz cans, black beans
2, 14.5oz cans, diced tomatoes
2, 4.5oz cans, chopped green Chiles
1 large sweet onion, diced
1 green bell pepper, diced
4 garlic cloves, minced
12oz can your favorite beer
1 packet, chili seasoning kit

Garnish: shredded cheddar cheese, diced tomatoes and avocado, sour cream, sliced green onions, and chopped fresh cilantro

Saute' steak in hot oil in a large skillet over medium-high heat for 5 minutes or until browned. Place steak in a lightly greased large crock-pot; stirring in black beans, sliced tomatoes, green Chiles, onion, bell pepper, and can of beer. Stir in packets from chili kit, omitting Masa and red pepper packets. Cover and cook on low for 10 hours. Serve with desired toppings.

TACO BAKE

2 lbs, taco meat
2 cans, enchilada sauce
1 package, flour tortillas
4 cups, shredded sharp cheddar cheese
2 large tomatoes, sliced
1 cup lettuce, chopped
2 cups, sour cream
Bottle of chives for shaking

Layer in large crock-pot, 1 lb taco meat, 1 can enchilada sauce, ½ package flour tortillas, 2 cups shredded sharp cheddar cheese, 1 large sliced tomato, ½ cup lettuce, 1 cup sour cream, and shake chives over top to taste. Repeat a second layer; cooking in slow cooker on low for 4 hours.

TATER TOT CASSEROLE

1 lb, ground beef, browned
1 can, Ro-Tel tomatoes, mild
1 lb package, frozen tater tots
1 can, cream of mushroom soup
1 medium onion, diced
16 slices, American cheese

Brown ground beef w/chopped onions, adding Ro-Tel
tomatoes. Pour beef and onion mixture on the bottom of a
greased crock-pot. Mix in cream of mushroom soup, topping
with tater tots across the top. Cook on low for 4 hours;
adding sliced cheese 30 minutes before serving.

ZESTY ITALIAN BEEF

4 lb, butt roast
1 bottle, Mezzetta's Italian Giardiniera mix
2 packets, zesty Italian salad and dressing mix
2 cans, beef broth

Place all in crock-pot and simmer for 10 hours, until beef falls apart.

- Serve w/your favorite hoagie buns.

MAIN DISHES

BAKED CRESCENT ROLL SANDWICHES

Cooking spray, for baking sheet
2 cans, crescent roll dough
½ lb, deli ham, sliced
¼ lb, pepperoni, sliced
¼ lb, provolone cheese, sliced
¼ lb, mozzarella cheese, sliced
1 cup, Pepperoncini peppers, sliced
2 Tbsp, olive oil
¼ cup, grated parmesan
1 tsp, dried oregano

Preheat oven to 350 degrees, and grease 9x13 glass baking dish w/cooking spray.

Unroll one can of crescents onto greased baking sheet and pinch seems together; layering with ham, pepperoni, provolone, mozzarella, and Pepperoncini. Unroll second crescent dough and place on top of Pepperoncini. Pinch together crescent sheets to seal. Brush olive oil all over top of crescent dough, and sprinkle parmesan and oregano on top.

Bake until crescent dough is golden and cooked through, about 30 minutes. If the crescent dough is browning too quickly, cover with foil.

Let cool for 15-20 minutes before slicing into squares.

BAKED RAVIOLI

1 lb, ground beef
24oz jar, marinara sauce
¼ cup, basil leaves, chopped
¼ cup, parsley, chopped
1 package, refrigerated cheese ravioli
16oz bag, shredded mozzarella cheese
2 Tbsp, grated parmesan

Set oven to 350 degrees. Coat a 2 quart oval baking dish with non-stick cooking spray. Bring a large pot of lightly salted water to a boil. Crumble ground beef into a large non-stick skillet. Cook for 5 minutes over medium-high heat, until browned. Remove from heat and stir in 1 cup of the marinara sauce, half the basil and half the parsley. Meanwhile, cook ravioli for 5 minutes in boiling water. Drain and return to pot. Stir in remaining sauce, basil and parsley. Pour half the ravioli into prepared dish, spreading level. Top with meat and sauce and ¾ cup of the shredded mozzarella. Add remaining ravioli to dish and top with remaining 1-1/4 cups shredded mozzarella and parmesan. Bake at 350 degrees for 25 minutes. Increase oven temperature to broil; broil ravioli for 5 minutes. Garnish with additional chopped basil, if desired.

BURRITO CASSEROLE

1 lb, ground beef
1 can enchilada sauce
1 can, sliced black olives, drained
1 can, diced tomatoes w/Chiles
8 burritos, frozen of your choice
9x13 baking pan

Garnish: shredded lettuce, and sour cream.

Cook ground beef, and drain. Mix in enchilada sauce, olives, diced tomatoes, and heat until hot. Layer burritos in 9x13 baking pan, add sauce mix over top. Heat oven to 375 degrees, and bake for 40 minutes. Remove from oven; adding shredded cheese over top, replace in oven for 15 minutes. After placing portions onto plates, add shredded lettuce and sour cream for garnish.

CHEESEBURGER CASSEROLE

1 lb, ground beef, cooked and drained
1 can cheddar cheese soup
1 can, cream of mushroom soup
1 lb, frozen crinkle fries
9x13 baking pan

Place ground beef in 9x13 baking pan, adding cheddar cheese soup and cream of mushroom soup. Slightly blend. Add crinkle fries over the top. Bake at 375 degrees for 35 minutes.

CHEESEBURGER FRIES

1 lb, ground beef
1 can, cream of mushroom soup
1 can, cheddar cheese soup
16oz bag, frozen crinkle cut fries

- Casserole dish

Preheat oven to 350 degrees. Fry ground beef in skillet; draining grease. Add soups to ground beef, and mix well. Place in bottom of casserole dish; topping with frozen fries.

Bake for 30 minutes. Can add shredded mozzarella cheese if desired.

CHEESEBURGER PIE

1 lb, ground beef
1 cup, onion, chopped
½ tsp, salt
1 cup, shredded cheddar cheese
1 cup, milk
½ cup, Bisquick baking mix
2 eggs

Preheat oven to 400 degrees. Cook ground beef and onion, and drain. Stir in salt. Spread meat mixture into greased 9" pie pan, and sprinkle with cheese. Stir remaining ingredients with fork until blended, and pour over top. Bake 30 minutes or until knife comes out clean when inserted.

CHEESY TOMATO MEAT BAKE

1 lb, ground beef
1 tsp, chili powder
1 cup, sour cream
2/3 cup, salad dressing
1 cup, sharp shredded cheddar cheese
2 Tbsp, onion, chopped
2 cups, Bisquick mix
½ cup, cold water
3 medium tomatoes, thinly sliced
¾ cup, green bell pepper, chopped

Preheat oven to 400 degrees. Spray 9x13 inch pan w/cooking spray. In large skillet, cook beef and chili powder over medium heat 8 minutes, stirring occasionally, until cooked. Drain beef, and set aside. In a small bowl, mix sour cream, salad dressing, cheese, and onions; setting aside. In medium bowl, stir in Bisquick mix and cold water with fork, until soft dough forms. Using fingers dipped in Bisquick mix to press dough in bottom, and ½ inch up sides of pan; layering beef, tomatoes, and bell pepper on dough. Place sour cream mixture over top, spreading evenly over vegetables to cover. Bake uncovered 30 minutes, or until edges of dough are light brown.

CHICKEN & RICE BAKE

1 can, cream of mushroom or chicken soup
1 cup, water or milk
¾ cup, white rice, uncooked
¼ tsp paprika
¼ tsp black pepper
6 chicken breast; skinless & boneless

Preheat oven to 375 degrees. Mix soup, water, rice, paprika, and pepper in bowl, until blended. Place chicken in bottom of 9x13 baking dish. Cover with soup mixture. Bake for 1 hour.

CHICKEN & STUFFING BAKE

4 cups, herb seasoned stuffing
6 chicken breast; skinless & boneless
1 Tbsp, paprika
1 can, cream of mushroom or chicken soup
1/3 cup, milk
1-1/4 cup, water
4 Tbsp, butter

Garnish: parsley

Set oven to 400 degrees. Mix stuffing w/1-1/4 cup boiling water, and 4 Tbsp butter. Spread across center of 9x13 glass casserole dish. Place chicken on each side. Sprinkle w/paprika. Mix soup and milk together; pouring over chicken. Cover and bake for 45 minutes, or until chicken is no longer pink inside.

CHICKEN AND RICE CASSEROLE

2 cups, chicken, canned w/juice
2 cups, French green beans, drained
1 can, cream of celery soup
1 cup, salad dressing
1 small yellow onion, chopped
1 box, wild rice; prepared as directed on box

Preheat oven to 350 degrees. Mix chicken, green beans, soup, salad dressing, onion, and rice together. Pour into a casserole dish. Bake for 45 minutes.

CHICKEN BACON RANCHG CASSEROLE

3 cups, chicken breast, cubed
2, 12oz cans, evaporated milk
1oz packet, hidden valley ranch dry mix
6 slices bacon, chopped
1/3 tsp, pepper
Salt to taste
1 lb, penne pasta, cooked as directed
2 cups, shredded cheddar cheese
1 cup, shredded Monterey jack cheese

Preheat oven to 350 degrees. Combine evaporated milk, ranch dressing, and pepper in heavy saucepan. Cook over low heat, stirring frequently, until dry ingredients are dissolved. Simmer, uncovered, 25 minutes, stirring frequently. Sauce will thicken slightly. While simmering sauce; fry bacon in small pan until crisp; 8 minutes. Remove from pan, and drain on plate w/paper towels. Cook pasta, and chicken most of the way. Combine all in a large bowl, until blended. Spray 9x13 glass baking dish, spreading ingredients into dish. Top with cheese; cover w/foil, and bake 45 minutes.

CHICKEN CASSEROLE

3 large cans, dark & white meat chicken breast, chopped
1 can, water chestnuts, drained
1 small can, sliced mushrooms w/juice
1 cup, mayonnaise
½ cup, celery, chopped
1 can, cream of mushroom soup
1 Tbsp, instant onions, diluted

Topping: 1 stick of butter, and 1 package chicken stove top stuffing.

Preheat oven to 325 degrees. Mix all ingredients, excluding topping ingredients, in a large bowl. Place in a 9x13 glass baking dish. Melt butter in sauce pan, adding stuffing mix until coated; placing on top of chicken mixture. Bake 1 hour, covering last 15 minutes to prevent over browning.

CHICKEN CHEESE MORNAY

1-1/2 Tbsp, butter
1-1/2 Tbsp, flour
¾ cup, half and half
½ cup, Swiss cheese, grated
Salt and pepper to taste
4 boneless; skinless chicken breast
½ cup, all-purpose flour
2 Tbsp, olive oil
4 slices bacon, cooked and diced
1 medium tomato, diced
1 Tbsp, parsley, chopped

In s small saucepan, melt butter. Whisk in 1-1/2 Tbsp flour. Whisk in half and half and heat until steaming. Whisk in cheese until melted. Simmer for 20 minutes, stirring often. Simmer oil in a skillet. Dredge the chicken in the flour. Add chicken to the pan and cook for 15 minutes, turning once. Top chicken with sauce; garnish with bacon, tomatoes and parsley.

CHICKEN MUSHROOM CASSEROLE

1 can, cream of mushroom soup
12 oz container, sour cream
Salt to taste
Pepper to taste
1 packet, Italian seasoning
1 tsp, garlic salt
2 cans, evaporated milk
1 Tbsp, butter, softened
1-1/2 cup, white or brown rice, uncooked
3 large cans, chicken breast
1 can, sliced mushrooms, drained
½ bag, flour tortillas
2 cups, shredded mozzarella

Preheat oven to 375 degrees. Grease 9x13 glass casserole dish. Add to large bowl, cream of mushroom soup, sour cream, salt, pepper, Italian seasoning, and garlic salt; mix together, adding evaporated milk. Mix and set aside. Add to casserole dish; butter-softened, spreading over bottom, uncooked rice, chicken breasts, and mushrooms. Pour soup mixture over top, then layer with flour tortillas; slicing to fit. Top w/shredded mozzarella cheese. Bake 1 hour covered, then 5 minutes uncovered to brown. Let sit 15 minutes before serving.

CHICKEN SOUR CREAM BAKE

4 each, chicken breast
1 container, sour cream
1 can, cream of mushroom soup
1 can, cream of chicken soup
1 box, chicken stuffing mix
1-2/3 cup, water

- 9x13 glass baking dish

Set oven to 350 degrees. Place chicken breasts in 9x13 dish. Mix cream of mushroom and cream of chicken soups together and pour over chicken. Mix chicken stuffing mix with water and pour over soup mix. Bake uncovered for 1 hour.

CHICKEN TETRAZZINI

12 oz box, Fettuccine
1 stick, butter
½ cup, all-purpose flour
4 cups, milk
1 cup, chicken stock
2 cups, parmesan cheese, divided
4 cups, canned chicken breast, white & dark meat
1 cup, sliced mushrooms
1 Tbsp, black pepper

Preheat oven to 350 degrees. Put pasta on to boil as directed. In medium sauce pan, melt butter on medium heat; stirring in four and cooking for 1 minute. Stir in milk, black pepper, chicken stock, and 1 cup parmesan cheese. Cook 1 minute, stirring constantly. Remove from heat; combining chicken breast chunks, and mushrooms. Let set 1 minute. When pasta is ready, drain; combining with other ingredients. Grease 9x13 baking dish lightly; placing mixture in dish, and topping with 1 cup of parmesan cheese. Cook for 45 minutes. Let stand 10 minutes before serving.

CHILI PIZZA

1 lb, ground beef
1 packet, schilling chili seasoning mix
1 can, stewed tomatoes
1 can, red kidney beans
2 cups, shredded cheddar cheese or mozzarella
1 can, black olives
8 large, flour tortillas

- Large pizza pan

Preheat oven to 400 degrees. Brown ground beef. Stir in seasoning mix, tomatoes, and kidney beans; heating until bubbly. Arrange tortillas on pizza pan, overlapping as needed. Cover w/meat mixture; topping with shredded cheese and black olives.

Bake 15 minutes, or until cheese is melted.

CHRIS'S MEAT LOAF

2 lbs, ground chuck
1 packet, dry onion soup mix
2 eggs, beaten
¼ cup, milk
¾ sleeve, crackers, crushed
8 slices, white bread, cut into small pieces
1 can, Hunt's organic diced tomatoes

Place all ingredients into a large mixing bowl; mixing with hands until well blended.

Preheat oven to 325 degrees. Place meat loaf into well greased 9x13 baking pan. Cook for 1.5 hours; draining grease. Let stand 10 minutes, cut & serve.

CORNED BEEF / CABBAGE CASSEROLE

3 medium red potatoes, sliced
1 stick, butter
1 small cabbage, chopped
1 bag, French fried onions
2 Tbsp, salt
2 Tbsp, pepper

- 9x13 Casserole dish

Preheat oven to 400 degrees. Spray casserole dish w/cooking spray. Layer x 2; cabbage, potatoes, salt, pepper, and ½ stick butter. Cover dish; baking in oven for 45 minutes. Remove from oven; removing cover. Top w/French fried onions; returning to oven for another 15 minutes. Remove from oven; letting stand 15 minutes before serving.

CREAMY BEEF CASSEROLE

1 lb, ground beef, cooked and drained
¼ cup, scallions, chopped
2 cans, tomato sauce
16oz package, egg noodles, boiled 5 minutes
8oz package, cream cheese, mixed w/sour cream
1 cup, sour cream, mixed w/cream cheese
2 cups, shredded mozzarella cheese

- 9x13 baking dish

Preheat oven to 375 degrees. Layer 9x13 baking dish as follows: ½ ground beef, noodles, cheese mix, then ½ ground beef. Top with mozzarella cheese, and cook for 30 minutes.

CRESCENT ROLL BAKE

2 cans, large crescent rolls
2 cups, shredded cheddar cheese
1 can, Sloppy Joe
1 lb, ground chuck
1 can, cream of mushroom soup
¼ cup, milk
1 can, sliced potatoes
1 can, green beans
1 cup, butter, melted
½ cup, parmesan cheese

- 9x13 baking pan

Preheat oven to 375 degrees. Cook ground chuck; draining grease. Mix with cream of mushroom soup, Sloppy Joe, potatoes, and green beans until well blended. Grease 9x13 baking dish; placing 1 roll of crescents in bottom of pan. Pour meat mixture over crescent roll w/2 cups shredded cheddar cheese. Place 1 of crescent rolls over top. Brush butter over top; sprinkling parmesan cheese on top. Bake for 35 minutes, or until heated and golden brown.

DEB'S MEATLOAF

2 lbs, lean ground beef or turkey
1 box, stove top stuffing, any variety
2 large, eggs, beaten
½ cup, barbecue sauce (I use Sweet Baby Ray's)
1 cup, water

- Optional: Ro-Tel tomatoes and Lipton onion soup mix

Preheat oven to 375 degrees. Line a 9x13 baking dish with foil; coating with nonstick spray. Mix meat, water, stuffing mix, and ¼ cup barbecue sauce in a bowl until well blended. Shape into oval loaf; placing into baking dish. Brush with remaining ¼ cup barbecue sauce. Bake 1 hour and 15 minutes, or until cooked through and a meat thermometer inserted in center registers at least 160 degrees.

DEEP FRIED CHICKEN

3 lb bag, chicken pieces
1 box, Kentucky kernel seasoned flour
1 box, Drake's Crispy Frymix
4 cups, whole milk
4 large, eggs, beaten

- Deep fryer, 2 large bowls, and large baking sheet

Heat deep fryer to 325 degrees. Mix Kentucky kernel seasoned four, and Drake's Crispy Frymix in large bowl. Mix milk and eggs in another large bowl. Dip 2 pieces of chicken at a time in flour bowl, then in milk bowl; repeat. Lay on baking sheet for 5 minutes. Place up to 6 pieces of chicken into deep fryer, cooking for 13.5 minutes. Remove chicken and place on serving dish lined with paper towels to remove excess grease.

DORITO CASSEROLE

2 lbs, ground beef
2 cans, cream of mushroom soup
2 cans, Ro-Tel tomatoes w/green Chiles
1 large bag, nacho cheese Doritos
4 cups, shredded cheddar cheese
½ cup, yellow onion, diced
1 Tbsp, salt
1 Tbsp, pepper

- 9x13 baking pan

Preheat oven to 350 degrees. Brown ground beef w/onion, salt and pepper; draining grease. Mix cans of Ro-Tel tomatoes, and cream of mushroom soup in a bowl. Place ½ of meat mixture in bottom of baking pan, layer with soup mixture, then Doritos. Add 2nd layer, then top with shredded cheddar cheese.

Bake in oven for 25 minutes.

EASY LASAGNA

2 lbs, hamburger meat
2 cans, pasta sauce
1 can, water from pasta sauce
2 box, oven ready noodles
1 Tbsp, minced garlic
4 cups, leaf spinach
4 cups, cottage cheese
4 cups, pizza blend shredded cheese
2 cup, grated parmesan
1 large, onion, diced

- Large glass baking dish

Preheat oven to 400 degrees. Brown ground beef in large skillet w/minced garlic, and onions. Drain grease. Mix pasta sauce w/meat mixture. Layer x 3; meat mixture, oven ready noodles; mixing in a criss-cross fashion, leaf spinach, cottage cheese, parmesan, then pizza blend shredded cheese. Cook in 400 degree oven for 1 hour.

EASY MEATLOAF

2 lbs, ground beef
16oz bag, favorite stuffing mix
2 large eggs, beaten
1 cup, water
1 cup, cattlemen's barbecue sauce, divided
1 packet, Lipton onion soup mix
1 can, Ro-Tel tomatoes

Heat oven to 350 degrees, mix all ingredients together in a large bowl w/1/2 cup cattlemen's barbecue sauce. Place aluminum foil on a flat baking sheet. Place meatloaf in an oval form onto baking sheet, then brush top with ½ cup cattlemen's barbecue sauce. Cook for 1 hour; letting cook for 15 minutes before serving.

EASY PARMESAN CHEESE BAKE

2 chicken breast, thawed & cut up
24oz can spaghetti sauce
1 tsp, minced garlic
1 tsp, basil
½ cup, parmesan cheese
½ bag, Texas toast croutons
2 cups, shredded Italian 4-cheese blend

Preheat oven to 350 degrees. In medium baking dish, place chicken breast in bottom. Mix spaghetti sauce, garlic, basil, and parmesan cheese until well blended; placing over top of chicken. Add ½ of Texas toast croutons, then shredded Italian four cheese blend.

Bake uncovered 30 minutes, then cover and bake 20 minutes.

EASY SLOPPY JOE BISCUIT PUFFS

1 can large, flakey refrigerated buttermilk biscuits
1 lb, ground beef
1 small onion, chopped
1 Tbsp, minced garlic
2 stalks, celery, finely chopped
1 small green pepper, chopped
1 Tbsp, salt
1 Tbsp, pepper
¾ cup, favorite barbecue sauce
1/3 cup, grated parmesan cheese
2 cups, grated mozzarella cheese

Preheat oven to 400 degrees. Prepare 10 un-greased standard-size muffin cups/tins. In a large skillet, brown ground beef with onion, garlic, celery, and bell pepper for 10 minutes or until beef is no longer pink; draining fat and adding salt and pepper to blend. Add barbecue sauce and simmer 15 minutes, stirring occasionally. Meanwhile, place 1 biscuit in each un-greased muffin tins and press the dough down firmly onto the bottoms and sides of the cups. Spoon ¼ cup of beef mixture into each biscuit cup. Sprinkle the tops with parmesan cheese and bake for 12 minutes or until the edges are golden brown. Remove from oven and sprinkle grated mozzarella cheese over tops of each biscuit; returning to oven for 2 minutes or until the cheese is melted. Let stand for 3 minutes; loosening edges of biscuits cups before removing from the pan.

ENCHILADA CASSEROLE

18oz bag, Doritos, save 2 cups for topping
1 large onion, chopped
14oz can chili w/beans
15oz can enchilada sauce
8oz can tomato sauce
2 cups, shredded cheddar

Topping:

2 cups, Doritos, crushed
1 cup, shredded cheddar
1-1/4 cup sour cream

Set oven to 375 degrees. In large glass casserole dish, add Doritos to bottom of dish; layering with chopped onion, chili w/beans, enchilada sauce, tomato sauce, and shredded cheddar. Cook for 30 minutes. Add 2 cups crushed Doritos, then sour cream, and 1 cup shredded cheddar to top; placing back to oven for 15 minutes, or until cheddar cheese is melted.

ERIC'S HOMEMADE MEATLOAF

2 lbs, ground beef
1 can, cream of mushroom soup
2 large eggs, beaten
¼ cup, self rising flour
15oz bottle, fancy ketchup, for topping
2 packets, Lipton's onion soup mix, 1 pack for topping
½ cup, Worcestershire sauce
15oz can tomato sauce
2 sleeves, saltine crackers, crumbled
1 cup, instant oatmeal
2 Tbsp, garlic powder
Dehydrated minced onions, to taste

Set oven to 350 degrees. Grease large glass or Pyrex baking dish. In large mixing bowl, add all ingredients in order, excluding ketchup, and 1 packet Lipton's onion soup mix. Place meat mixture in baking dish, forming loaf. Cover top with ketchup; sprinkling 1 packet Lipton's onion soup mix. Place in oven for 1.5 hours; removing to cool for 20 minutes before cutting to serve.

FARMER'S CORNBREAD CASSEROLE

1 lb, ground beef
1 can, beef barley soup
1 can, cream of mushroom soup
1 can, whole yellow corn, drained
1 can, green beans, drained
1 can, diced potatoes, drained
1 box, Zatarain's jalapeno cornbread
3 cups, shredded cheddar (reserving 1 cup for Zatarain's)

- 9x13 baking pan

Set oven to 375 degrees. Grease 9x13 baking pan with butter or Pam spray. Mix Zatarain's jalapeno cornbread mix per instructions on box. Pour into glass baking dish, and shake dish to even cornbread mix. Cook for 15 minutes, or until cornbread stands. Pull from oven and poke holes in top of cornbread with end of spatula. Brown ground beef in medium sauce pan. Add beef barley soup, cream of mushroom soup, corn, green beans, and diced potatoes until hot. Pour meat/soup mixture over top of cornbread, and add 2 cups of shredded cheddar over top of meat/soup mixture. Place into preheated oven for 30 minutes.

Let stand 15 minutes before cutting to serve.

FRENCH ONION CHICKEN NOODLE

4 cups, chopped chicken
2 cans, cream of mushroom soup
16oz container, French onion dip
1 cup, shredded cheddar
12oz, egg noodles
1 cup, French fried onions, crushed for topping

- 9x13 baking pan

Preheat oven to 350 degrees. Cook noodles per packet instructions. Spray 9x13 baking pan with cooking spray. Combine all ingredients, excluding French fried onions, into large mixing bowl; blending well. Place mixture into baking pan. Top with French fried onions. Bake 45 minutes.

FRITO PIE

2 cans, tamales, drain; saving juice
2 cans, chili w/beans
½ cup, onion, diced
1 bag, Fritos corn chips
10 slices, American cheese

- Medium glass baking dish

Preheat oven to 350 degrees; lightly greasing. Layer x 2, in baking dish. 1 can of tamales, 1 can of chili w/beans, ¼ cup onion, ½ bag of Fritos, and 5 slices of American cheese. When finished, pour saved tamale juice over top. Place in oven for 30 to 45 minutes, or until cheese is melted to a golden brown.

GOULASH

46oz can tomato juice
2 lbs, hamburger
1 large onion, diced
2 cans, diced tomatoes w/green chilies
½ box, beef stock
½ bottle, Clamato juice
2 cups, elbow macaroni
2 packets, Lipton onion soup mix

Fry hamburger in large stock pot with onion, and Lipton soup mix. Do not drain grease. Add tomato juice, diced tomatoes w/green chilies, beef stock, Clamato juice, and elbow macaroni; bringing pot to a boil; reducing heat to simmer. Cook for 1 hour.

GRILLED CHICKEN

4 each, chicken breast
4 chicken thighs
4 packets, dry Italian dressing mix
4 cups, olive oil
2 cups, apple cider vinegar

- Outdoor grill

In medium bowl, mix dry Italian dressing mix, olive oil and apple cider vinegar; blending well. In large air tight container, place chicken, covering with marinate. Cover, and refrigerate for 4 to 6 hours. Place chicken pieces, wrapped in tin foil on preheated outdoor grill at 350 degrees. Grill for 30-35 minutes, or until chicken is cooked to 165 degrees, utilizing a meat thermometer.

HAMBURGER CASSEROLE

1 lb, hamburger
1 can, sliced potatoes, drained
1 can, sliced carrots, drained
1 can green beans w/juice
1 medium onion, diced and sautéed
1 can, cream of mushroom soup
1 can evaporated milk
2 cups, shredded cheddar

- Large glass baking dish

Set oven to 400 degrees. In a large skillet; brown hamburger w/onion; draining grease. Mix in sliced potatoes, carrots, and green beans; heating until bubbly. In medium bowl, mix cream of mushroom soup and evaporated milk until well blended. Place hamburger mixture in large glass baking dish, topping with soup mixture. Place in oven and bake for 45 minutes. Remove from oven and top with shredded cheddar; returning to oven for 15-20 minutes, or until cheese is melted.

ITALIAN BOW TIE PASTA

16oz package, bow tie pasta
1 lb, Italian sausage
½ cup, onion, chopped
2 tsp, minced garlic
½ tsp, crushed red pepper flakes
2, 14.50z cans, Italian stewed tomatoes
2 cups, heavy whipping cream
1 tsp, salt
1 tsp, dried basil
1 tsp, pepper
2 cups, shredded parmesan cheese

Cook pasta according to package directions. In a Dutch oven, cook the sausage, onion, and pepper flakes over medium heat for 10 minutes or until sausage is no longer pink. Add garlic; cooking 5 minutes; draining grease. Chop tomatoes, adding to sausage mixture w/whipping cream, salt, basil, and pepper. Bring to a boil over medium-low heat. Reduce heat to a simmer, uncovered for 10 minutes or until thickened, stirring occasionally. Drain pasta, and toss into sausage mixture; blending well. Garnish w/parmesan cheese.

LASAGNA

1 box, oven ready lasagna noodles
16oz container, ricotta cheese
4 each, Roma tomatoes, thinly sliced
1 lb, ground beef
1 large can spaghetti sauce
1 small onion, diced
2 cups, shredded mozzarella cheese

- 9x9 baking dish

Preheat oven to 375 degrees. Grease baking dish and set aside. Brown ground beef w/onion, draining grease. Place ground beef in bottom of baking dish, layer with oven ready noodles, ricotta cheese, tomatoes, then top with spaghetti sauce. Cook for 45 minutes, removing from oven and topping with mozzarella cheese. Return to oven for 10-15 minutes, or until mozzarella is melted.

LASAGNA PIE

1 lb, ground beef
½ cup, cottage cheese
1 cup, shredded mozzarella cheese
½ tsp, salt
½ tsp, oregano
6oz can tomato paste
1 cup, whole milk
2 eggs, beaten
¾ cup, Bisquick baking mix
Optional; parmesan cheese to taste

- 12-inch pie plate

Preheat oven to 425 degrees. Spread cottage cheese in greased pie plate. Cook ground beef; draining liquid. Stir in ½ cup of mozzarella cheese, salt, oregano, and tomato paste; blending well and spreading over cottage cheese. In medium mixing bowl, stir in milk, eggs, and baking mix with fork until well blended; pouring over mixture. Bake 45 minutes, or until knife in center comes out clean. Sprinkle w/remaining cheese, returning to oven for 5 minutes or until melted. Sprinkle w/parmesan cheese, if desired, before serving.

LINKED CHILI DOG CASSEROLE

1 lb, ground beef
2 cloves garlic, minced
1 medium bell pepper, diced
1 large onion, diced, ½ divided
4 Tbsp, chili powder
½ tsp, pepper
1 tsp, salt
1 Tbsp, sugar
6oz can tomato paste
1 cup, water
2 cups, shredded mozzarella cheese
10 each, pork hotdogs, cut in half

* Garnish: Prepared mustard, and parmesan cheese.
* 9x9 inch pan

Set oven to 400 degrees. In large skillet, fry ground beef w/garlic, bell pepper, diced onion, chili powder, pepper, and salt. Drain fat. Add sugar, tomato paste, and water; mixing until blended. Simmer for 45 minutes. Place hot dogs on bottom of 9x9 inch pan, and cover with chili sauce mix. Place cheese over chili, topping with ½ divided onions. Bake for 30 minutes, removing from oven to set for 10 minutes. Top with dollops of prepared mustard, and parmesan cheese if desired.

MAC & CHEESE PIE

20oz box, Penne or Rotini pasta
½ stick, butter
32oz block, Velveeta cheese, chunked
16oz package, Mexican blend shredded 4-cheese
16oz package, mild shredded cheddar
5 large eggs, beaten
1 tsp, salt
1 tsp, pepper
1 cup, milk
1 cup, bread crumbs

- 9x13 baking pan

Preheat oven to 400 degrees. Cook pasta according to directions. Grease baking pan w/Pam spray. Add ½ of pasta to bottom of dish. Spread chunks of Velveeta on top of pasta. Add ½ of Mexican 4-cheese and ½ of mild cheddar.

Add rest of pasta, then rest of cheeses. Mix eggs with salt, pepper, and milk; pouring over top of pasta mix. Top with bread crumbs. Bake; covered loosely for 1 hour; removing lid last 15 minutes of baking time.

MAHI-MAHI

4 each, Mahi-Mahi fillets
1 packet, McCormick all-purpose breading
1 cup, parmesan shredded cheese

- Flat baking sheet

Preheat oven to 425 degrees. Do not grease baking sheet. Place McCormick's all-purpose breading in a large bowl. Dip Mahi-Mahi in breading until covered. Place Mahi-Mahi onto baking sheet, sprinkling w/parmesan cheese. Bake for 35 minutes.

MAUDIE'S MEXICAN MEAT LOAF

2 lbs, 93/7 ground beef
½ cup, diced onion
1 Tbsp, diced garlic
½ tsp, sea salt
½ tsp, black pepper
¼ tsp, cayenne pepper
1 Tbsp, chili powder
¾ cup, bread crumbs
2 large eggs, slightly beaten
8oz can tomato sauce

Topping:

½ cup, catsup or ketchup
½ tsp, chili powder
¼ cup, brown sugar

- 9x13 glass baking dish

Preheat oven to 350 degrees. Mix all ingredients for meatloaf; shaping into loaf. Place in baking dish; cooking for 45 minutes. Remove from oven; topping with sauce mixture and spreading evenly. Return to oven for 20 minutes, until top glazes. Topping should be made while meatloaf is cooking so flavor will meld together.

MEXICAN BAKE

2 each, jumbo burritos, sliced
2 cans, enchilada sauce
1 can chili w/beans
1 can, black beans, drained
1 box, jambalaya rice, cooked
4 cups, shredded cheddar

- 9x13 glass baking dish

Preheat oven to 375 degrees. Place ¾ can enchilada sauce on the bottom of baking dish, adding chili w/beans; spreading to cover. Add drained can of black beans to cover, jambalaya rice to cover, then ¼ can of enchilada sauce. Cover w/2 cups shredded cheddar.

Place sliced burritos over top of dish; pouring 1 can enchilada sauce over top, covering with other 2 cups of shredded cheese.

Cover w/foil; baking 45 minutes to an hour. Remove from oven; letting sit for 15 minutes before serving. Serve w/dollops of sour cream.

MEXICAN HAMBURGER CASSEROLE

1 lb, ground beef
8oz package, cream cheese, chunked
2 cups, mild chunky salsa
2 cups, sharp shredded cheddar cheese

In medium skillet, fry ground beef. Add cream cheese & salsa; heating until boiling. Reduce heat to a simmer; adding shredded cheddar until melted.

* Serve over rice or egg noodles.

MEXICAN LASAGNA

2 lbs, hamburger
1 small onion, chopped
2 cans, enchilada sauce
2 cans, refried beans
2 packages, shredded Mexican 4-cheese blend
1 small can, black olives
2 medium tomatoes, chopped
6 large, flour tortillas cut to fit pan
2 packets, taco seasoning

Garnish: cold lettuce, sour cream, and favorite vegetables.

- 9x13 baking pan

Preheat oven to 350 degrees. Cook hamburger and onions in large skillet. Add taco seasoning and olives, and reheat. Set aside. Cover bottom of baking dish w/thin coating of enchilada sauce; adding flour tortillas to cover. Heat 1 can of refried beans and layer over flour tortillas, along with a layer of enchilada sauce, meat mixture, shredded cheese blend, and tomatoes. Repeat layers. Add layer of flour tortillas, enchilada sauce, and cheese to top. Bake for 45 minutes to 1 hour, making sure heated thoroughly. Top w/cold lettuce, sour cream and vegetables to taste.

MEXICAN TORTILLA PIZZA

8 each, flour tortillas
1 can refried beans
2 cups, Mexican 4-cheese blend
½ cup, taco sauce
1 cup, shredded lettuce
1 cup, diced tomatoes
Diced onion for garnish, if desired
Sour cream for garnish, if desired

- - Large, cookie sheet

Preheat oven to 400 degrees. Put 4 tortillas on un-greased baking sheet. Spread thin layer of refried beans on tortillas. Sprinkle ¼ cup cheese blend on each tortilla. Place another tortilla on top of cheese. Press down on top tortilla. Top with remaining cheese. Bake 8 minutes. Remove from oven. Spread tortillas with taco sauce, lettuce and tomatoes. To serve, cut each into 4 wedges. Top with sour cream and onion, if desired.

MOM'S CREAM CHICKEN

4 chicken breast, removing skin
1 can, cream of mushroom soup
1 can, cream of chicken soup
1 large onion, diced
½ stick, butter

Boil chicken breast in a 6 quart sauce pan for 35 minutes or until done; removing chicken and reserving 1 cup of broth. Sautee onion in small sauce pan w/butter. Shred chicken w/fork and return to pot, stirring in cream of mushroom soup, cream of chicken soup, sautéed onions, and cup of broth. Bring to a boil; removing from heat. Let cool 15 minutes before serving.

* Serve w/fresh buttered biscuits, mashed potatoes, or egg noodles.

OVEN FRIED CHICKEN

8 assorted, chicken pieces
2 cups, all-purpose flour
2 tsp, Lawry's season salt
½ tsp, dried basil
1 tsp, dried oregano
1 tsp, black pepper
1 tsp, garlic powder
2 cups, buttermilk
2 each, large eggs
¾ cup, canola oil

* Broiler pan or 9x13 baking pan
* 2 large mixing bowls

Preheat oven to 400 degrees. Mix flour, Lawry's season salt, basil, oregano, pepper, and garlic powder until well blended. In 2nd bowl, mix buttermilk and eggs until yellowish in color. Dip chicken pieces in milk mixture, then coating w/flour mixture. Pour canola oil in bottom portion of broiler pan; adding chick pieces. Bake in oven 30 minutes, turning once; returning to oven to bake an additional 30 minutes.

PASTA ALA JJ

1 lb, ground beef
1 small onion, diced
1 small green bell pepper, diced
16oz package, provolone shredded cheese
16oz package, Monterey jack & Colby shredded cheese
1 can spaghetti sauce
1 small can, tomato sauce
1 can diced tomatoes
1 small can, sliced black olives
16oz package, Wacky-Mac macaroni

- Casserole dish

Preheat oven to 375 degrees. Fry ground beef w/onion and bell pepper in medium skillet. Drain grease. Add spaghetti sauce, tomato sauce, diced tomatoes, and sliced black olives to ground beef; bringing to a boil. Cook macaroni per package instructions and mix with meat sauce. Pour into casserole dish, topping with shredded cheeses.

Bake 30 minutes or until cheese is melted.

PASTA JAMBALAYA

20oz bag, penne pasta
1 can Ro-Tel tomatoes
1 lb package, polish or smoked sausage, chopped
1 jar, Alfredo sauce
3 dollops, sour cream
1 Tbsp, garlic powder
½ jar, sliced sweet red peppers
1 cup, grated pepper jack cheese
Papa Murphy's pizza seasoning to taste
Papa Murphy's red pepper flakes to taste
Parsley flakes to taste

Cook pasta per package instructions, and drain. Add all ingredients, excluding grated pepper jack cheese, to large skillet; simmering 25-30 minutes. Remove from heat; letting sit for 5 minutes. Top with grated pepper jack cheese.

Serves well w/Texas toast.

PEPPER PASTA

¼ cup, olive oil
4 oz, pepperoni slices, cut in half
2 green bell peppers, cored and cut into strips
2 red bell peppers, cored and cut into strips
1 medium onion, thinly sliced
3 cloves garlic, minced
1 lb box, linguini, cooked according to package directions

In large skillet, heat oil over medium heat. Add pepperoni slices, peppers, onion, and minced garlic; cook, stirring until vegetables are soft. About 5 minutes. Add drained linguini to skillet; tossing to coat evenly.

Serves well w/garlic toast.

PORK TENDERLOIN W/RICE

8 pieces, pork tenderloin
1 can, cream of mushroom soup
1 can, cream of chicken soup
1 can, cream of celery soup
1 can, beef Consommé
1 can, French onion soup
¾ stick, butter
1-1/2 cup, long grain brown rice
2oz package, slivered almonds

Set oven to 275 degrees. Melt butter and add to rice, until blended. Place rice in bottom of large skillet. Place pork tenderloin over rice. Mix all soups in large bowl, until blended well. Pour soup mixture over tenderloins; adding slivered almonds to top.

Bake in oven for 3 hours.

POTATO CASSEROLE

2 lbs, frozen hash brown
1 stick butter, melted
2 cups, grated cheddar cheese
½ cup onion, chopped
2 cups, sour cream
1 can, cream of chicken soup
3 cups cornflakes, crushed

* 9x13 baking pan

Preheat oven to 350 degrees. Melt ½ stick butter in 9x13 baking pan. In a large bowl, combine potatoes, cheese, onion, sour cream, and soup. Mix well, and place in baking pan. Stir remaining butter into crushed corn flakes, and sprinkle over potatoes. Bake 1.5 hours.

* This recipe can be made ahead of time and refrigerated over night. Bring to room temperature before baking.

PRIME RIB ROAST

1 each, 3.5lb prime rib roast, well marbled
1 stick, butter
1 packet, McCormick's brown gravy mix
1 packet, McCormick's au jus mix
2 tsp, garlic powder
2 tsp, Lawry's season salt
1 tsp, ground black pepper
½ cup, kosher salt

Preheat oven to 500 degrees. Bring prime rib roast to room temperature, around 4 hours; rubbing w/kosher salt. Mix in bowl; butter, brown gray mix, au jus mix, garlic powder, season salt and black pepper, until well blended. Cover prime rib roast w/butter topping. Place roast on broiler pan in center rack of oven; cooking 20 minutes. Turn oven off and let roast sit in oven for 2 hours. Serve with au jus.

* DO NOT OPEN THE OVEN DOOR FOR ANY REASON *
* PRIME RIB ROAST WILL BE TO PERFECTION *

RIBLET SURPRISE

1 package, barbecue rib-lets, microwave as directed, sliced
6 each, jumbo buttermilk biscuits
1 cup, shredded cheddar cheese
1 cup, cattlemen's barbecue sauce

- Standard 6 cup muffin pan

Preheat oven to 375 degrees. Spray muffin pan w/Pam or butter spray. Place biscuits in muffin slots, pressing to sides and bottom. Add rib-lets to biscuit muffin; dollop w/barbecue sauce, and topping w/shredded cheddar cheese.

Bake for 20-25 minutes.

RICE CASSEROLE

1 box, Zatarain's garlic butter rice, cooked as directed
16oz package, white cheddar cheese w/Mediterranean herb
2 each, country fried steaks, thawed
1 bag, pepper stir-fry
½ stick, butter

Add butter to medium fry-pan, cooking country fried steaks; cutting into pieces. Add steaks to rice. Sautee' pepper stir-fry; adding to rice and meat, and bring to a simmer; cooking 15 minutes. Top w/cheese and serve.

ROUND STEAK

1 large round steak, tenderized
2 can, golden mushroom soup
¾ can, water
1 small onion, diced
2 Tbsp, canola oil
2 Tbsp, Lawry's season salt
1 Tbsp, ground black pepper

Set oven to 350 degrees. Cook round steak on high w/canola oil, and diced onion in skillet. Mix golden mushroom soup w/water, Lawry's seasoning salt, and black pepper; placing over round steak. Cover skillet and bake in oven for 2 hours.

SANTA FE SKILLET CHICKEN

1 large onion, chopped
1 Tbsp, butter or margarine
1-1/4 cups, chicken broth or stock
1 cup, chunky salsa
1 cup, long grain rice, uncooked
½ tsp, garlic powder
4 each, boneless chicken breast halves
¾ cup, shredded cheddar cheese

Optional: Fresh cilantro or parsley.

In a large skillet, sauté onion in butter until caramelized. Add broth and salsa; bring to a boil. Stir in rice and garlic powder. Place chicken over rice; cover and simmer for 10 minutes. Turn chicken; cook 15 minutes longer or until meat juices run clear. Remove from the heat. Sprinkle w/cheese; cover and let stand 5 minutes. Garnish w/cilantro or parsley if desired.

SEVEN LAYER CASSEROLE

½ cup, uncooked rice, washed & drained
1 cup, whole kernel corn, drained
1 tsp, salt
1 tsp, pepper
1 can tomato sauce
1 cup water
½ cup green bell pepper, finely chopped
½ cup yellow onion, finely chopped
1 lb, ground beef, cooked and drained
4 slices, bacon

- 2 quart casserole dish

Preheat oven to 350 degrees. In casserole dish, place in layers; rice, corn, salt, pepper, and spread with ½ can tomato sauce mixed with ½ cup of water. 2nd; layer onion; green pepper and ground beef. Sprinkle with salt and pepper. Mix ½ can tomato sauce; with ½ cup water, and pour over top. Cover casserole mixture w/bacon slices cut in half. Cover skillet and bake for 1 hour. Uncover and bake 30 minutes longer.

Top w/shredded mozzarella cheese if desired.

SHEPHERD'S PIE

2 lbs, hamburger
1 large onion, diced
1 cup peas, drained
1 cup, creamed corn
1 cup, carrots, chopped
Instant mashed potatoes, prepared as directed

- Large casserole dish

Preheat oven to 350 degrees. Cook hamburger w/diced onion; draining grease. Mix peas, creamed corn, and carrots to hamburger; mixing until well blended. Place in casserole dish and bake for 30 minutes.

Serve on top of mashed potatoes.

SLOPPY JOE CASSEROLE

2 lbs, ground beef
1 large onion, diced
2 cans, Manwich or favorite sloppy joe mix
1 can red kidney beans w/liquid
2 large cans, crescent rolls
2, 16oz bags, Mexican 4-cheese blend

- Casserole dish

Set oven to 375 degrees. Brown ground beef w/onion; and drain grease. Add Manwich and kidney beans to meat; reheating until hot. Spray casserole dish with Pam or butter spray. Spread 1 can of crescent roll in bottom of casserole dish. Pour meat mixture over crescent roll. Add 2nd can of crescent rolls; spreading over meat mixture. Top w/cheese blend. Bake in oven for 20-25 minutes, until golden brown.

SPAGHETTI CHICKEN
(By Verna)

4 each, chicken breast; boneless-skinless, thawed
1 jar, Prego traditional spaghetti sauce
½ box, spaghetti noodles
2 Tbsp, olive oil
1 cup, shredded mozzarella cheese

- Casserole dish

Preheat oven to 350 degrees. Take chicken breast and place in bottom of casserole dish; covering w/spaghetti sauce. Bake 40 minutes or until chicken is done.

While chicken is cooking, cook spaghetti noodles on stove per box instructions; draining water, and adding olive oil so not to stick.

When chicken breast finish cooking; sprinkle shredded mozzarella cheese over each breast; returning to oven until cheese is melted.

To serve: Spoon up spaghetti noodles on your plate; add chicken breast on top of spaghetti noodles, cover w/spaghetti sauce, and sprinkle w/mozzarella cheese.

Serve with garlic bread or a lettuce salad.

SPAGHETTI PIE

1 lb, ground beef, browned w/greased drained
2, 8oz cans, zesty tomato sauce
1-1/2 cup, sour cream
2 oz package, cream cheese, softened
4 cups, long spaghetti, cooked and drained
1 small onion, diced
1-1/3 cup, shredded cheddar cheese

- Casserole dish

Set oven to 350 degrees. Brown ground beef w/diced onions in medium skillet draining grease. Mix in tomato sauce; bring to a boil and simmer 15 minutes. Spray casserole dish w/Pam spray or butter. Place ground beef mixture in bottom of casserole dish. Next, add the long spaghetti. Mix the sour cream and cream cheese until blended; adding to top of spaghetti. Sprinkle with shredded cheddar cheese.

Bake for 40 minutes, making sure all is heated through, and cheese is melted.

Serve with cheese bread.

SPAGHETTI PIZZA DELIGHT

16oz box, long spaghetti
2 eggs, beaten
3-1/2 cups, mozzarella cheese, shredded
¾ tsp, garlic powder
½ tsp, salt
32oz can spaghetti sauce
1-1/2 tsp, oregano
16oz bag, sausage crumble toppings
7oz bag, pepperoni slices
4oz container, Portobello mushroom slices
2.25oz can, black olive slices

- Large cookie sheet

Preheat oven to 400 degrees. Cook spaghetti, drain and rinse in cold water. Add eggs, ½ cup mozzarella cheese, garlic powder and salt. Mix well and put onto well greased cookie sheet. Bake for 15 minutes at 400 degrees. Remove from oven and top w/spaghetti sauce, remaining mozzarella cheese, oregano, sausage crumbles, pepperoni slices, mushrooms, and black olives.

Reduce oven to 350 degrees; cooking pizza until cheese is melted.

STUFFED PEPPERS

1/3 cup, uncooked long-grain white rice
2/3 cup, water
4 large, green bell peppers
1 lb, ground beef
¼ cup, celery, chopped
2 Tbsp, onion, chopped
½ tsp, salt
1/8 tsp, pepper
¼ cup, ketchup
1 medium tomato, chopped
8oz can tomato sauce
1 tsp, sugar
¼ tsp, dried basil leaves
¼ cup, shredded cheddar cheese

Set oven to 350 degrees. Cook rice in water as directed on package. Cut tops from bell peppers; removing membrane and seeds. In large saucepan, bring enough water to cover peppers to a boil. Add peppers; cook over medium heat for 5 minutes. Drain; set peppers aside. In large skillet, combine ground beef, celery and onion; cook 10 minutes or until beef is thoroughly cooked, stirring frequently. Drain. Add cooked rice, salt, pepper, ketchup and tomato; mix well. Place mixture into peppers. Place peppers in un-greased, shallow baking pan. In small bow, combine tomato sauce, sugar and basil; mixing well. Spoon half of sauce over peppers. Bake for 40 minutes or until peppers are tender, spooning remaining sauce over peppers and sprinkling with cheese last 10 minutes of baking.

TANGY TILAPIA

¼ cup, grated parmesan cheese
2 Tbsp, mayonnaise
1 Tbsp, butter, softened
1 Tbsp, lime juice
1/8 tsp, garlic powder
1/8 tsp, dried basil
1 tsp, ground black pepper
1 tsp, onion powder
6 each, tilapia fillets
¼ tsp, salt

In a small bowl, combine parmesan cheese, mayonnaise, butter, lime juice, garlic powder, dried basil, black pepper, and onion powder; mixing well. Set aside. Line a broiler pan with foil, and coat foil with cooking spray. Place fillets in prepared pan; sprinkle w/salt.

Broil 3 minutes on each side. Spread 1 tablespoon of cheese mixture over top of each fillet. Broil 3 minutes longer, or until topping is golden brown.

Serve with homemade garlic/butter biscuits.

TATER TOT CASSEROLE

1.5 lbs, ground beef
16oz bag, tater tots, seasoned
1 can, cream of mushroom soup
10 slices, Velveeta cheese
1 large onion, diced

- Casserole dish

Set oven to 325 degrees. Spray casserole dish w/cooking spray. Cook ground beef w/onions in large skillet; draining grease. Place ground beef in bottom of casserole dish. Add 5 slices of Velveeta cheese. Spread cream of mushroom soup over Velveeta cheese. Add seasoned tater tots to cover. Add 5 more slices of Velveeta cheese over casserole.

Bake for 1 hour and 10 minutes. Let stand 15 minutes before slicing to serve.

TUNA TETRAZZINI

12oz box, fettuccine
1 stick, butter
½ cup, all-purpose flour
4 cups, whole milk
1 cup, dill pickle juice
2 cups, parmesan cheese, divided
4 cups, tuna chunks
1 cup, water chestnuts, sliced
1 Tbsp, black pepper
1 Tbsp, salt

- 9x13 baking pan

Set oven to 350 degrees. Put pasta on to boil as directed via packet. In medium sauce pan; melt butter on medium heat; stirring in flower; cooking 1 minute. Combine, milk, black pepper, salt, pickle juice, and 1 cup parmesan cheese. Cook 1 minute, stirring constantly. Remove from heat; combining tuna and water chestnuts. Let set 1 minute. When pasta is ready, drain, combine with other ingredients. Grease 9x13 baking pan lightly; placing mixture in pan, topping w/1 cup parmesan cheese.

Bake for 45 minutes. Let stand 10 minutes, before serving w/favorite breads.

WEDGE SEASONED CASSEROLE

½ bag, potato wedges, seasoned
2 lbs, ground beef
1 can, cream of mushroom or cream of chicken soup
1 packet, Lipton Onion Soup mix
1 cup, sour cream
6 slices, American sliced cheese
3 cups, shredded cheddar cheese

* 9x13 glass baking dish

Preheat oven to 425 degrees. Place potato wedges in bottom of casserole dish; baking for 18 minutes. While wedges are baking, fry ground beef in large skillet; adding cream of soup, Lipton Onion Soup mix, and sour cream; bringing to bubbly heat.

Remove potato wedges from oven, pouring meat mixture over wedges; adding sliced cheese over top, and spreading shredded cheddar over sliced cheese.

Reduce heat to 350 degrees; returning to oven for 30 minutes.

ZESTY ITALIAN CRESCENT CASSEROLE

1 lb, ground beef
1 medium onion, minced
1 cup, spaghetti sauce
1-1/2 cups, sharp shredded cheddar cheese
½ cup, sour cream
1 large can, buttery crescent rolls
1/3 cup, grated parmesan
2 Tbsp, melted butter

- Casserole dish

Set oven to 375 degrees. Spray casserole dish w/Pam spray.
Fry ground beef w/onions in skillet; draining grease. Place ½
ground beef in bottom of casserole dish. Pour ½ cup
spaghetti sauce over ground beef. Mix sharp cheddar cheese
and sour cream together; placing ½ of mixture over
meat/sauce mixture. Repeat 2nd layer as first. Roll out
crescent dough; adding to top of mixture. Mix together
parmesan cheese and melted butter; placing over top of
casserole.

Bake in oven for 18 to 25 minutes; making sure crescent roll is
golden brown.

ZITI TACO CASSEROLE

1 box, ziti pasta
1 lb, ground beef
1 packet, taco seasoning
1 small jar, taco sauce
1 cup, water
12oz container, cream cheese
2 cups, Mexican 4-cheese shredded cheese
1 medium onion, diced

- 9x13 cake pan

Set oven to 325 degrees. Spray cake pan w/cooking spray.
Cook ziti 9 minutes, and drain. Brown ground beef w/onion in
skillet draining grease. Add taco seasoning, water, and cream
cheese to meat; simmering 15 minutes. Place cooked ziti in
bottom of cake pan; topping with 2 cups of shredded cheese.
Add ground beef mixture; mixing gently. Sprinkle with taco
sauce, and topping with rest of shredded cheese.

Bake in oven for 30 minutes.

DESSERTS

2-INGREDIENT PINEAPPLE CAKE

1 box, yellow cake mix
1 large can, crushed pineapple w/juice

- 9x13 baking pan

Preheat oven to 350 degrees. In large bowl; combine yellow cake mix and pineapple w/juice. Stir by hand; the mixture will start to froth, becoming fluffy and airy.

Spray baking pan w/Pam spray. Pour cake mix into baking pan; baking for 30 minutes.

Remove from oven and let cool before cutting to serve.

10 MINUTE APPLE CRISP

8 medium, tart apples, peeled and sliced
¾ cup, brown sugar, divided
½ cup, all-purpose flour, divided
¾ cup, quick-cooking oats
1 tsp, ground cinnamon
½ cup, cold butter, cubed

Toss apples with ¼ cup brown sugar and 2 Tbsp all-purpose flour; place in a greased 8-inch microwave-safe, deep-dish pie plate. In a bowl, combine oats, cinnamon and remaining brown sugar and flour. Cut in butter until crumbly; sprinkle over apple mixture. Cover with waxed papers. Microwave on high 10 minutes or until apples are tender.

ALMOND CARAMEL CANDY

1 cup, granulated sugar
½ cup, brown sugar
½ cup, light corn syrup
1-1/2 cups, half and half
6 tbsp, butter
1 tsp, vanilla
½ cup, chopped toasted almonds

* 9x5x3 inch loaf pan

Spread bottom and sides of loaf pan with butter. In 2-quart saucepan, combine granulated sugar, brown sugar, corn syrup, half and half, and the 6 Tbsp of butter or margarine. Cook and stir over medium heat till sugars dissolve. Continue cooking, stirring occasionally, to firm ball stage. Remove from heat; stir in vanilla and almonds. Turn into prepared pan; cool. Cut into squares; wrap each w/wax paper.

APPETIZING EGGNOG TREATS

2 cups, sugar
1 cup, dairy eggnog
1 Tbsp, Caro syrup
2 Tbsp, oleo
1 tsp, vanilla
½ cup, chopped candied cherries
½ cup, flaked coconut

- 8x8 inch loaf pan

Butter sides of a 5-quart saucepan. In prepared pan combine sugar, eggnog, and Caro syrup. Cook over medium heat, stirring constantly, until the mixture comes to boiling. Cook to soft ball stage, without stirring. Immediately remove from heat; cool to lukewarm, without stirring. Add oleo and vanilla. Beat vigorously till very thick and candy just starts to lose its gloss, about 10 minutes. Quickly stir in cherries and coconut; pour into buttered loaf pan. Let cook, and cut into squares.

APPLE CAKE

3 eggs, beaten
¾ cup, vegetable oil
2 cups, sugar
2 cups, flour
1 tsp, vanilla
3 cups, chopped apples (peeled)
1 cup, nuts or pecans
1 tsp, cinnamon
½ tsp, nutmeg

- 9x13 baking pan

Preheat oven to 350 degrees. Combine oil, sugar, eggs, and vanilla in mixing bowl, and mix well. Add flour, apples, nuts or pecans, cinnamon, and nutmeg. Mix and pour into greased baking pan. Bake at 350 degrees for ½ an hour, then 325 degrees for ½ an hour.

BROWN SUGAR TOPPING FOR APPLE CAKE

1 cup, brown sugar
1 stick, butter
¼ cup, milk

Mix all ingredients in medium saucepan, cooking for 5 minutes. Cool and pour over cake.

CARAMEL DRIZZLE FOR APPLE CAKE

14oz can sweetened condensed milk
1 cup, firmly packed brown sugar
2 Tbsp, butter

½ tsp, vanilla extract

In a medium saucepan, combine milk, and brown sugar; bringing to a boil over medium-heat, whisking constantly. Reduce heat, and simmer for 10 minutes, whisking constantly. Remove from heat; whisk in butter and vanilla. Let cook 5 minutes. Drizzle over cake in 9x13 baking pan.

Let cool before cutting to serve.

APPLE CRISP

2 eggs, beaten
1-3/4 cup, sugar
2 heaping, tsp cinnamon
½ cup, oil
6 medium, Gala, Fuji, or Honey Crisp apples
2 cups, flour
2 tsp, baking soda

- 9x13 baking pan or 2-9" round pans

Preheat oven to 350 degrees. In a large bowl, mix eggs, sugar, cinnamon, and oil. Peel and slice apples; adding to mixture in bowl, coating as you go to keep apples from turning brown. Mix together baking soda, and flour; adding to ingredients in bowl. Mix well, best with a fork, until all the flour is absorbed by the wet ingredients. Pour mixture in greased 9x13 baking pan or two 9" round pans.

Bake for 55 minutes. Let cool ½ an hour before cutting to serve.

BANANA PUDDING

1 can, Eagle Brand Milk
1 cup, ice cold water
6 bananas, peeled and sliced
1 box, vanilla pudding
1 box, banana pudding
1 quart, whipping cream
1 box, shortbread cookies

- glass serving dish

In a separate bowl, beat whipping cream for 2 minutes. In another bowl, mix together cold water, Eagle Brand Milk, and both packages of pudding mixes. Scrape bowl of whipping cream in with the other mixed ingredients; stirring well, until completely blended. Slice bananas. In a serving dish, layer bananas, shortbread cookies, and pudding. Sprinkle top w/crushed shortbread cookies.

Place in refrigerator to chill before serving.

BANANA PUDDING CHEESECAKE

1-1/2 cups, crushed vanilla wafers
20 each, vanilla wafers
1 cup, coarsely crushed vanilla wafers
½ cup, chopped pecans
½ cup, melted butter or margarine
2 diced, bananas
1 sliced, banana
1 Tbsp, lemon juice
2 Tbsp, brown sugar
24oz container, cream cheese
1 cup, granulated sugar
3 eggs, beaten
2 Tsp, vanilla extract

- 1 round cake pan and 1 medium sauce pan

Preheat oven to 250 degrees. Place 1-1/2 cups of crushed vanilla wafers and ½ cup chopped pecans into mixing bowl. Add ½ cup melted butter, and mix until blended. Place into bottom of round cake pan; flattening out. Place 20 vanilla wafers around the edges of the round cake pan, pressing down into crust mixture. Bake for 10 minutes.

Place diced bananas and lemon juice in saucepan; heating until mixed. Add brown sugar, reheating until mixed. Let stand.

Place cream cheese in mixer; blend until smooth. Add sugar, eggs, vanilla, and mix w/mixer until blended smoothly.

Place banana mixture and cream cheese mixture into bowl; blending together. Place into round cake pan; baking at 350 degrees for 45 minutes. Let cool. Shake coarsely crushed vanilla wafers over the top, adding 5 dollops of whipped cream. Add 1 sliced banana and 1 vanilla wafer to each dollop of whipped cream.

Cool in refrigerator for 1 hour. Slice and serve.

BANANA LAYER DESSERT

3 cups, cold milk
1 box, vanilla or cheesecake flavored instant pudding mix
8oz can, crushed pineapple, drained
1 each, prepared angel food cake, cut into cubes
1 cup strawberries, sliced with ¼ cup sugar on them
8oz container, frozen whipped topping, thawed
2 medium bananas, sliced
¼ cup, pecans, chopped
12oz jar, hot fudge microwaveable topping

Whisk milk and pudding for 2 minutes in large bowl. Stir in pineapple. Place half of the angel food cubes on the bottom of a large, clear class bowl. Spread 1/3 of pudding mixture on top. Cover w/sliced strawberries. Spread layer of whipped topping over strawberries. Remove lid from hot fudge topping and heat in microwave on high for about 30 seconds. Pour half the fudge over the previous layer and then add a layer of cake cubes. Spread another 1/3 of pudding mixture on top. Cover with sliced bananas, then remaining pudding mixture. Spread whipped topping over all. Drizzle w/fudge topping and sprinkle w/pecans. Chill until serving. Garnish w/strawberries and bananas when serving.

CINNAMON PECAN PUFFS

¾ cup, chopped pecans
½ cup, butter
½ cup, firmly packed light brown sugar
3 Tbsp, corn syrup
2 tsp, ground cinnamon, divided
8oz can, large buttered crescent rolls
2 tsp, granulated sugar

• 12-inch round cake pan

Preheat oven to 350 degrees. Bake pecans and butter in lightly greased round cake pan for 5 minutes. Swirl pan to combine, and bake 5 more minutes. Remove from oven, and stir in brown sugar, corn syrup, and 1 tsp cinnamon; spread mixture over bottom of pan. Unroll crescent roll dough, and separate into 4 rectangles, pressing perforations to seal. Stir together granulated sugar and remaining 1 tsp cinnamon; sprinkle over rectangles. Roll up each rectangle tightly, starting at 1 long side; press edges to seal. Cut each log into 4 slices; place slices into prepared pan. Do not let slices touch.

Bake for 20 minutes or until golden brown. Remove from oven, and immediately invert pan onto a serving dish. Pour topping over rolls.

BLUEBERRY ESKIMO ICE CREAM

2 cups, Crisco
2 cups, granulated sugar
8 cups, blueberries, frozen

In large bowl, add Crisco and sugar. Mix well w/hands for approximately 10 minutes. Fold in blueberries until mixed well w/out crushing berries.

Ice cream is now ready to eat.

BUTTER FROSTING

2 cup, butter
2, 16oz package, powdered sugar
½ cup, milk
2 tsp, vanilla extract

Cook butter in a small saucepan over medium heat, stirring constantly, 10 minutes or until butter begins to turn golden brown. Remove pan from heat immediately, and pour butter into small bowl. Cover and chill 2 hours. Beat butter at medium speed w/an electric mixer until fluffy; gradually adding powdered sugar alternating with milk, beginning and ending w/powdered sugar. Beat mixture at low speed until well blended after each addition. Stir in vanilla.

Frosting is ready for cake.

BUTTERMILK CUSTARD PIE

1-1/2 cup, granulated sugar
¼ cup, all-purpose flour
½ cup, butter, softened
3 eggs, beaten
½ tsp, vanilla
½ tsp, salt
½ cup, buttermilk
1 unbaked pie shell, 9-inch

- 9-inch round pie pan

Set oven to 350 degrees. Mix sugar and flour; cream w/butter. Add eggs, vanilla, salt and buttermilk. Gently pour into pie shell and bake for 30 minutes, or until filling is set.

Let cook 1 hour before slicing to serve.

BUTTERSCOTCH NUTTY FUDGE

12oz package, butterscotch pieces
14oz can sweetened condensed milk
2 cups, tiny marshmallows
1 cup, chunk-style peanut butter
1 tsp, vanilla
1 cup, chopped peanuts

- 9x9x2-inch pan

In saucepan, combine butterscotch pieces, milk, and marshmallows. Stir over medium heat till marshmallows melt. Remove from heat; beat in peanut butter, vanilla, and dash of salt. Stir in nuts. Pour into butter pan. Chill; cutting into squares.

Refrigerate 1 hour.

CAPPUCCINO OREO PIE

4oz box, instant vanilla pudding and pie filling
2 cups, cold milk
3 tsp, instant coffee
1-1/2 cups, prepared whipped topping, divided
1 each, Oreo pie crust
2 Tbsp, almond slivers

* 9-inch pie pan

Prepare pudding mix according to package directions using milk and coffee. Fold in 1 cup prepared whipped topping. Pour into crust. Chill for 4 hours.

Top w/whipped topping and almond slivers before serving.

CARAMEL COCONUT PIE

½ cup, butter or margarine
12oz bag, flaked coconut
1 cup, chopped pecans
12oz container, cream cheese, softened
1 can Eagle Brand milk
12 oz jar, caramel topping
2 each, 9" frozen pie shells
16oz, container Cool Whip

- 2 each, 9-inch round pie pans

Melt butter or margarine in a large skillet; add coconut and pecans. Cook; stirring constantly until golden brown; set aside. Combine cream cheese and Eagle Brand milk; beat until smooth, fold in Cool Whip. Layer a 1/2 cream cheese mixture in each pie shell. Drizzle half caramel topping on top of each pie. Spread half coconut-pecan mixture over each pie. Repeat layers; cover and freeze. Remove from freezer 15 minutes before serving.

CARAMEL PECAN DELIGHT

16oz package, pecan cookies, crushed
½ cup, butter or margarine, melted
2 each, 8oz packages cream cheese, divided
12oz jar, caramel ice cream topping, divided
1-1/2 cups, cold milk
1 box, instant vanilla pudding mix
¾ cup, chopped pecans

- 9x13 baking pan

Set oven to 375 degrees. In a bowl, combine cookie crumbs and butter. Press into greased baking pan. Bake for 10 minutes. Cool on a wire rack.

In a large bowl, beat cream cheese and ½ cup caramel topping until smooth. In a bowl, whisk milk and pudding mix for 2 minutes; folding into cream cheese mixture. Spread over cooled crust. Sprinkle w/pecans.

Cover and refrigerate for at least 6 hours. Cut into squares; drizzle w/remaining caramel topping.

CARAMEL POPCORN

Roaster pan full of popped popcorn
2 cups, brown sugar
½ cup, light Caro syrup
1 cup, butter
½ tsp, salt
½ tsp, baking soda

- Roaster pan

Preheat oven to 250 degrees. Mix brown sugar, Caro syrup, butter, and salt in large saucepan; boiling for 5 minutes. Remove from heat; adding soda and stirring well. Pour over popcorn; placing roaster in oven, baking for 1 hour, stirring every 15 minutes.

Let cool; serving w/vanilla ice cream.

CHERRY CROCK-POT DESSERT

1 large can, cherry pie filling
2 boxes, Jiffy cake mix
1 stick, butter
Pam or butter spray
Cool Whip, optional

Spray Crock-Pot w/Pam or butter spray. Place cherry pie filling in bottom of Crock-Pot. Melt butter and mix w/Jiffy cake mix; placing in Crock-Pot over cherry pie filling.

Cook on low for 3 hours. Enjoy w/dollops of Cool Whip.

CHEX BUTTERSCOTCH BARS

8 cups, Chex cereal
2 cup, light corn syrup
1-1/2 cup, sugar
2 cups, crunchy peanut butter
3 cups, semi-sweet chocolate chips
3 cups, butterscotch chips
½ cup, creamy peanut butter
2 tsp, vanilla extract

- 9x13 glass dish

Butter a large bowl, and measure out 8 cups Chex cereal. Set aside. Butter a 9x13 glass dish. In a small saucepan, combine the corn syrup over medium heat. Once boiling; immediately remove from heat and stir in 2 cups crunchy peanut butter. Pour over cereal and fold together. Pour cereal into the 9x13 glass dish, using hands to press together.

Melt chocolate chips, butterscotch chips, ½ cup creamy peanut butter and vanilla in microwave; heating in 15 second intervals, stirring between to prevent the chocolate from burning.

Once smooth; pour over cereal. Allow to cool completely before slicing to serve.

CHOCOLATE BUNDT CAKE

1 box, chocolate cake mix
1 package, instant chocolate pudding
3 Tbsp, baking cocoa
1-3/4 cup, milk
2 eggs, beaten
12oz bag, semi-sweet morsels
Powdered sugar for dusting of cake

- Bundt cake pan

Preheat oven to 350 degrees. Spray Bundt cake pan w/Pam or butter spray. In large bowl, mix together; cake mix, instant chocolate pudding, baking cocoa, milk, and eggs w/mixer for 2 minutes; adding morsels ¼ of a bag at a time. When blended, pour into Bundt cake pan.

Bake for 60 minutes, or until toothpick comes out clean.

Let cake cool before shaking w/powdered sugar. Slice and serve.

CHOCOLATE MORSEL CHEESECAKE

2 rolls, refrigerated chocolate chip cookie dough
4 each, 8oz packages, cream cheese, softened
1 cup, granulated sugar
4 eggs, beaten
1 tsp, vanilla extract

- 9x13 cake pan, greased; set aside

Preheat oven to 325 degrees. Take 1 roll of cookie dough, cut into slices and press into bottom of pan to form a crust. Mix cream cheese, sugar, eggs, and vanilla until smooth. Pour over cookie dough in pan. Take second roll of cookie dough, cut into slices and place on top of cheese cake mixture. Bake 1 hour.

Refrigerate 4 hours before serving.

CHOCOLATE CHERRY COOKIES

2 cups, all-purpose flour
½ cup, cocoa powder
¼ tsp, salt
¼ tsp, baking powder
¼ tsp, baking soda
½ cup, oleo, softened
1-1/2 cup, sugar
2 eggs, beaten
1-1/2 tsp, vanilla extract
10oz jar, Maraschino cherries
8oz package, semi-sweet chocolate pieces
¾ cup, Eagle Brand sweetened condensed milk

- Large cookie sheet

In a large bowl, stir together flour, cocoa powder, salt, baking powder, and baking soda. In mixer bowl, beat together butter or margarine and sugar on low speed of electric mixer till fluffy. Add eggs and vanilla; beat well. Gradually add dry ingredients to creamed mixture; beat till well blended. Shape dough into 1 inch balls; place on ungreased cookie sheet. Press down center of dough with thumb. Drain Maraschino cherries, reserving juice. Place a cherry in the center of each cookie. In small saucepan, combine chocolate pieces and sweetened condensed milk; heat till chocolate is melted. Stir in 4 tsp of reserved cherry juice. Spoon about 1 tsp of frosting over each cherry, spreading to cover cherry. Frosting may be thinned w/additional cherry juice, if necessary.

Bake for 8 minutes; allowing to cool 30 minutes.

CHOCOLATE 4-LAYER DESSERT

* 9x13 cake pan

1st layer;

1 cup, all-purpose flour
1 stick, butter (1/2 cup)
½ cup, chopped pecans

Preheat oven to 325 degrees. Mix all ingredients together, pour into cake pan, bake for 15 minutes; cool.

2nd later;

1 cup, powdered sugar
8oz package, cream cheese, softened
1 container, Cool Whip

Place all ingredients into large bowl; mixing well. Pour over 1st layer.

3rd layer;

1 box, instant vanilla pudding
1 box, instant chocolate pudding
3 cups, cold milk

Place all ingredients into large bowl; mixing well. Pour over 2nd layer.

4th layer;

Add 1 container of Cool Whip and nuts over 3rd layer. Place in refrigerator to set over night before serving.

CHOCOLATE MARSHALLOW COOKIE PIE

2 cups, miniature marshmallows
2 Tbsp, milk
2-1/2 cups, Cool Whip
2 cups, cold milk
2 packages, instant chocolate pudding
1 each, chocolate pie crust
14 each, vanilla wafer cookies

- 9 inch round pie pan

Microwave marshmallows w/2 Tbsp milk on high for 45 seconds; stir and refrigerate 15 minutes. Stir in 1 cup Cool Whip to marshmallows; adding 2 cups milk into bowl. Add pudding packages; mixing well, letting stand 1 minute. Add 1-1/2 cups Cool Whip. Pour into crust.

Arrange cookies over mixture. Spread marshmallow mixture over cookies.

Refrigerate 4 hours. Drizzle w/chocolate topping just before serving, if desired.

CHOCOLATE MOUSSE

1 can, sweetened condensed milk
½ gallon, cold chocolate milk
8oz container, Cool Whip

In large bowl; mix all ingredients together and place in mousse serving dishes. Refrigerate for at least 4 hours before serving.

Serve w/cold Cool Whip, if desired.

CHOCOLATE NUTTER BUTTER DESSERT

16 each, Nutter Butter, sandwich cookies, divided
2 Tbsp, butter, melted
16oz package, cream cheese, softened
½ cup, crunchy peanut butter
¾ cup, sugar
2 tsp, vanilla
16oz container, Cool Whip, thawed and divided
3 squares, Baker's semi-sweet chocolate, melted

- 9x5 inch loaf pan

Crush 8 Nutter Butters in re-sealable plastic bag. Mix cookie crumbs and butter. Press onto bottom of 9x5 inch loaf pan.

Mix cream cheese, peanut butter, sugar and vanilla with electric mixer on medium speed until well blended. Gently stir in 4 cups of Cool Whip. Spoon ¾ cup of cream cheese mixture into a small bowl. Stir in melted chocolate until well blended; set aside. Spoon half of remaining cream cheese mixture over crust. Top evenly with chocolate mixture; cover with remaining cream cheese mixture.

Freeze 4 hours or overnight until firm. Invert onto plate. Remove foil, then re-invert onto serving platter so that crumb layer is on bottom. Coarsely break the remaining 4 Nutter Butters. Add Cool Whip and Nutter Butters over top.

CHOCOLATE PECAN BARS

1-1/2 cup, all-purpose flour
¾ cup, sugar
¾ cup, cocoa
¼ tsp, salt
1 cup, cold margarine
3 eggs, beaten
1 can, Eagle Brand sweetened condensed milk
2 tsp, maple flavoring
2-1/2 cups, pecan halves or pieces

- 9x14 cake pan

Preheat oven to 325 degrees. In large bowl, stir together; flour, sugar, cocoa, and salt; cut in butter until crumbly. Stir in 2 beaten eggs. Press mixture evenly on bottom of un-greased baking pan. Bake 35 minutes.

Meanwhile, in medium bowl, beat sweetened condensed milk, remaining 1 egg and flavoring; stir in pecan halves. Pour over prepared crust, distributing pecan halves evenly.

Return to oven; baking 35 minutes longer or until golden. Cool; cutting into bars.

CHOCOLATE PIE

9" Oreo or Graham Cracker crust
2 cups, sugar
¼ cup, cornstarch
¼ tsp, salt
3-1/2 cups, whole milk
3 egg yolks, beaten
8oz bag, bitter-sweet chocolate, finely chopped
2 tsp, vanilla extract
2 Tbsp, butter
Cool Whip for serving

Combine in medium saucepan; sugar, cornstarch, and salt. Stir or whisk together. Pour in milk and egg yolks, and whisk together. Stir over medium heat until the mixture just barely comes to a boil and becomes thick, about 10 minutes. When it starts to thicken; remove from heat. Add the chocolate, vanilla, and butter; stirring until everything is combined.

Pour the pudding in pie crust, put in the refrigerator to chill for 6 hours, loosely covered.

Serve w/Cool Whip.

CHOCOLATE CARAMEL CHEESECAKE

9" Oreo cookie crust
12oz package, caramels
½ cup, evaporated milk
1 cup, chopped pecans, divided
6oz container, cream cheese, softened
¾ cup, sour cream
1-1/2 cups, milk
1 box, instant chocolate pudding
1 cup, fudge topping

Place caramels and evaporated milk in a heavy saucepan. Cook over medium-low heat, stirring continually, until smooth, 10 minutes. Stir in 1 cup chopped pecans. Pour into piecrust.

Combine cream cheese, sour cream and milk in a blender; processing until smooth. Add pudding mix; processing for 1 minute.

Pour pudding mixture over caramel layer, covering evenly. Chill 30 minutes.

Drizzle fudge topping over pudding layer; sprinkling top of pie w/remaining pecans. Chill loosely cover, until serving time.

CHRISTMAS GELATIN CANDY

6 envelopes, un-flavored gelatin
3/4 cup, granulated sugar
3 cups, apricot juice
3 Tbsp, lemon juice

In 2-quart saucepan; combine gelatin and sugar. Add fruit juice; wait 1- minutes. Bring to boiling; reduce heat. Cook and stir till gelatin dissolves. Add lemon juice. Pour into shallow pans or paper baking cups. Cool; chill until firm. Cover pans or store cutouts in single layer, between waxed paper, in airtight containers up to 5 days.

Spiked Gelatin Candy: Prepare as above, except substitute bottled pina colada cocktail mix for the fruit juice.

COCOA REESE'S CHIP PIE

9oz packaged, Graham Cracker crumb crust
1 cup, Reese's peanut butter chips
¾ cup, butter or margarine
¼ cup, cocoa
1 can, Eagle Brand sweetened condensed milk
½ cup, water
1 egg, beaten
½ tsp, vanilla extract
Whipped topping, optional

Preheat oven to 350 degrees. Sprinkle chips on bottom of crust. In medium saucepan, over low heat; melt butter. Add cocoa, stir until smooth. Add sweetened condensed milk and water; stirring with whisk until well blended. Stir in egg and vanilla. Remove from heat, and pour into crust.

Bake 45 minutes or until done; center will become firm while cooling. Top w/whipped topping, if desired.

CREAM CHEESE FROSTING

8oz package, cream cheese, softened
4 Tbsp, butter, softened
2 cups, powdered sugar
½ tsp, salt
1-1/2 tsp, vanilla extract

Beat cream cheese and butter until smooth and creamy. Gradually add sugar and salt, beating until blended. Stir in vanilla.

DARK CHOCOLATE FROSTING

12oz package, semi-sweet chocolate morsels
½ cup, whipping cream
3 Tbsp, butter, softened

Microwave semi-sweet chocolate morsels and whipping cream together on medium powder 3 minutes or until chocolate begins to melt.

Whisk until chocolate melts and mixture is smooth. Whisk in butter; let stand 1 minute. Beat at medium speed w/an electric mixer 5 minutes or until mixture stiffens.

DARK FRUITCAKE

1 cup, oleo
4 cups, all-purpose flour
2 tsp, baking powder
3 tsp, ground cinnamon
½ tsp each, ground nutmeg, allspice, and cloves
1 tsp, salt
16oz, diced mixed candied fruits and peels
8oz package, pitted whole dates, snipped
8oz, whole green candied cherries
16oz package, raisins
1-1/2 cups, slivered almonds
1-1/2 cups, pecan halves
¾ cup, chopped candied pineapple
4 eggs, beaten
2 cups, packed dark brown sugar
1-1/2 cups, orange juice
½ cup, light molasses

- 2-9x9 inch loaf pans

Preheat oven to 275 degrees. Grease loaf pans. Line bottom and sides of pans with brown paper to prevent overbrowning; grease paper. In saucepan, melt oleo; cool. Stir together flour, baking powder, cinnamon, nutmeg, allspice, cloves, and 1 tsp salt. Add mixed fruits and peels, dates, cherries, raisins, almonds, pecans, and pineapple; mix until well coated. Beat eggs until foamy. Add brown sugar, orange juice, molasses, and oleo; beat until blended. Stir into fruit mixture.

Turn batter into prepared pans, filling each ¾ full. Bake for 3 hours; covering pans loosely w/foil after 1 hour. Place fruitcakes on wire racks; cooling 4 hours. Remove from loaf pans; refrigerating for 24 hours before slicing to serve.

DECADENT BROWNIES

1 box, brownie mix
1-1/2 cups, chunky peanut butter
2 cups, semi-sweet chocolate chips
1 cup, creamy peanut butter
3 cups, Rice Krispies cereal

- 9x13 cake pan

Set oven to 350 degrees. Grease cake pan w/butter. Bake brownie mix as directed on box side panel. Cool for 30 minutes. Spread chunky peanut butter over top of brownies. Melt semi-sweet chocolate chips w/creamy peanut butter; adding Rice Krispies to mixture; stirring until blended. Spread over top of chunky peanut butter.

Place in refrigerator and chill for 30 minutes before slicing to serve.

DEEP DISH APPLE COBBLER

* 9x13 cake pan
* Preheat oven to 350 degrees.

Crust and topping

1 package, yellow cake mix
1 cup, quick cooking oats
1 cup, chopped pecans
¾ cup, melted margarine

Mix all ingredients in large bowl, and divide. Sprinkle 1 bowl in bottom of cake pan.

Filling

7-1/2 cups, sliced apples
½ cup, water
½ cup, nuts
3 Tbsp, sugar
2 tsp, ground cinnamon
½ tsp, ground nutmeg

Mix all ingredients in large saucepan on low heat for 10 minutes; spreading over crust. Sprinkle other bowl of crust over top; baking for 35 minutes, until lightly browned.

Let cool for 1 hour before serving.

EASY CREAM CHEESE CAKE

1 box, cake mix – any flavor
3 large eggs, beaten
1 can, pie filling – any flavor
2 packages, cream cheese, chilled, chopped in squares

- 9x13 class baking dish

Preheat oven to 350 degrees. Grease baking dish w/Pam spray or butter. In large bowl, mix in dry cake mix, eggs, and pie filling. Stir together until well blended. Pour cake mix into baking dish. Place chopped cream cheese squares sporadically into cake mix; making sure cheese is covered. Bake for 35 minutes or until toothpick comes out clean.

Let cake cook before serving.

EASY MONKEY BREAD

24 each, frozen dinner rolls
1 large package, butterscotch pudding (not instant)
1 cup, butter
1 cup, brown sugar
3 tsp, cinnamon
¾ cup, chopped pecans

- Bundt cake pan

Preheat oven to 325 degrees. Butter bottom and sides of Bundt cake pan. Arrange rolls in bottom of pan. Sprinkle pudding over rolls. In saucepan; cook brown sugar, butter, and cinnamon until sugar melts. Add pecans and pour over rolls. Cover tightly and leaving on counter overnight.

Bake for 50 minutes; allowing to set for 15. Turn onto serving plate, and pull apart w/fingers.

FLOURLESS CHOCOLATE CAKE

4-1oz square, semi-sweet chocolate, chopped
8-1/2oz squares, Ghirardelli Caramel chocolate, chopped
½ cup, butter
¾ cup, white sugar
½ cup, cocoa powder
3 eggs, beaten
1 tsp, vanilla extract

- 8-inch round cake pan

Preheat oven to 300 degrees. Grease cake pan, and dust w/cocoa powder. Melt chocolate and butter in saucepan on low heat. Remove from heat; stirring in sugar, cocoa powder, eggs, and vanilla. Pour into prepared pan.

Bake for 30 minutes; letting cool in pan for 10 minutes. Turn out onto wire rack; cool completely. Slices can be reheated in microwave for 15 seconds before serving, if desired.

Serve with strawberries, raspberries, or blueberries, and dusting of powdered sugar.

FRESH HOMEMADE APPLE CAKE

1-1/2 cups, chopped pecans
½ cup, butter, melted
2 cups, sugar
2 large, eggs
1 tsp, vanilla extract
2 cups, all-purpose flour
2 tsp, ground cinnamon
1 tsp, baking soda
1 tsp, salt
4 large, Honey Crisp apples, peeled; cut into wedges

* 9x13 baking dish

Preheat oven to 375 degrees. Coat baking dish w/Pam spray, and set aside. Stir together; butter, sugar, and eggs in large mixing bowl, until blended.

Combine flour, ground cinnamon, baking soda, and salt; adding to butter mixture, stirring until well blended. Stir in apples and 1 cup of pecans; spreading batter into baking dish.

Bake for 50 minutes or until a toothpick inserted in middle of cake comes out clean. Cool completely in baking pan on wire rack.

Spread your choice of frosting over top of cake, sprinkling w/remaining pecans.

FRESH CINNAMON ROLLS

1 cup, chopped pecans
16oz package, hot roll mix
½ cup, butter – softened
1 cup, firmly packed dark brown sugar
2 tsp, ground cinnamon
1 cup, powdered sugar
2 Tbsp, cold milk
1 tsp, vanilla extract

- Large Cast-Iron Skillet

Prepare hot roll mix as directed. Let dough sit 10 minutes. Roll dough into a rectangle; spreading with softened butter. Stir together; brown sugar, and cinnamon; sprinkling over butter. Sprinkle pecans over brown sugar mixture; rolling up tightly, starting at one long end, and cut into 12 slices. Place rolls, cut side down, into greased Cast-Iron Skillet. Cover; put in warm place to rise, 30 minutes or until doubled in bulk.

Preheat oven to 400 degrees. Uncover rolls, and bake for 35 minutes or until center of rolls are golden brown. Let cool in pan on wire rack; 15 minutes. Stir together powdered sugar, milk, and vanilla extract; mixing well, drizzling over rolls.

Let set 5 minutes before serving.

GERMAN CHOCOLATE FLIP CAKE

1 cup, chopped pecans
1 cup, coconut
1 box, German Chocolate cake mix
8oz package, cream cheese, softened
1 lb package, powder sugar
1 tsp, vanilla extract
½ cup, butter, melted

- 9x13 cake pan

Preheat oven to 325 degrees. Grease cake pan, and set aside.
Sprinkle pecans and coconut over bottom of cake pan.
Prepare cake mix as directed on box. Pour batter over pecans
and coconut. Blend cream cheese and powdered sugar
together; carefully stirring in melted butter and vanilla
extract. Beat until well blended. Pour over top of cake batter,
and lightly spread.

Bake for 45 minutes, or until toothpick comes out clean. Turn
cake out upside down and leave pan over cake for 10 minutes,
allowing topping to loosen from pan.

Best served warmed.

GOOEY CAKE

1 box, yellow cake mix
1 stick, butter
4 eggs, beaten
1 box, Confectioner's Sugar
8oz package, cream cheese, softened

- 9x13 cake pan

Preheat oven to 300 degrees. Grease cake pan, and set aside. Beat together cake mix, butter, and 2 eggs. Spread in cake pan. In medium mixing bowl; combine Confectioner's Sugar, cream cheese, and 2 eggs; mixing until well blended.

Pour over cake mixture and bake 1 hour. Remove from oven; cooling on wire rack.

Cool over night in refrigerator, if desired before serving.

HAWAIIAN ICE CREAM

2 cans, Root Beer
1 can 7-up
1 can, sweetened condensed milk

Mix all ingredients in large bowl until well blended; freezing.
Take out of freezer every 2 hours and stir; refreezing. 10 hours
total.

HONEY BUN CAKE

Cake

1 box, yellow cake mix
4 eggs, beaten
¾ cup, canola oil
1 cup, buttermilk
1 cup, brown sugar
2 tsp, ground cinnamon
½ cup, pecans

- 9x13 cake pan

Preheat oven to 350 degrees. Grease cake pan, and set aside. Mix all ingredients, excluding brown sugar, ground cinnamon, and pecans, in large mixing bowl. Pour cake batter in cake pan. Mix brown sugar, ground cinnamon, and pecans in bowl; swirling into cake batter.

Bake fro 35 minutes. Remove from oven; letting cool.

Drizzle

1 cup, powdered sugar
2 Tbsp, cold milk
1 tsp, vanilla extract

Mix all ingredients together, until well blended; pouring over honey bun cake.

Let set 30 minutes before serving.

ICE CREAM PIE

1 stick, butter
1 cup, brown sugar
3 cups, Rice Chex, crushed
½ gallon, ice cream of choice

Melt butter; stirring in sugar slowly, in large mixing bowl. Add 2-1/2 cups crushed Rice Chex; folding twice. Press in pie pan; freezing 20 minutes. Soften ice cream; pouring over Rice Chex mixture. Sprinkle remainder ½ cup of Rice Chex over top of pie; returning to freezer for 30 minutes.

Remove from freezer 10 minutes before slicing to serve.

IF YOU LIKE MRS. FIELDS COOKIES

2 cups, sugar
2 cups, butter or oleo
2 cups, brown sugar
4 eggs, beaten
2 tsp, vanilla extract
4 cups, all-purpose flour
5 cups, dry oatmeal
1 tsp, salt
2 tsp, baking soda
24oz bag, chocolate chips
8oz Hershey bar, grated
3 cups, chopped nuts

- Un-greased large cookie sheet

Preheat oven to 375 degrees. Cream together; sugar, butter or oleo, and brown sugar. Add eggs, vanilla, flour, and oatmeal to mixer bowl, blending until powdered; adding to wet mixture. Add chocolate chips, Hershey bar, and chopped nuts; blending well, and making into golf ball size cookies. Flatten cookies w/a glass just a little on top; placing 2" apart on un-greased cookie sheet.

Bake 8-18 minutes, or lightly golden. Remove from oven and let cool before serving.

Yields 10 dozen cookies.

INSIDE CARO S'MORES

10 cups, Golden Grahams cereal
2 cups, milk chocolate morsels
8 cups, miniature marshmallows
6 Tbsp, butter or margarine
1 tsp, vanilla extract
1/2 cup, light Caro syrup

- 9x13 cake pan

Melt 8 cups marshmallows, (saving 2 cups for later), chocolate morsels, butter and Caro syrup in 5 quart saucepan over low heat, stirring occasionally. Remove from heat; stirring in vanilla extract, until well blended. Butter cake pan, and set aside. Pour Golden Grahams cereal into large bowl; adding marshmallows over cereal, stirring until coated. Stir in remaining marshmallows.

Press mixture into cake pan; letting cool completely.

Store covered at room temperature.

JELLO PUDDING PIE

2 boxes, instant chocolate or vanilla pudding, your choice
2-3/4 cup, cold milk
8oz container, Cool Whip
9", Graham Cracker pie crust

In large mixing bowl, beat milk, pudding, and ½ of Cool Whip w/whisk, until well blended; spreading into pie crust. Spread remaining Cool Whip over filling.

Refrigerate 24 hours for best taste, before serving.

JULIE'S CREAM PIE

2 cups, heavy whipping cream
14oz can sweetened condensed milk
½ cup, chocolate syrup
1 cup, mini marshmallows
½ cup, favorite nuts
½ cup, mini chocolate chips

- 2 each, empty Cool Whip containers

In large mixing bowl, beat whipping cream to stiff peaks. In separate bowl, mix sweetened condensed milk and chocolate syrup together; folding into whipping cream.

Add mini marshmallows, favorite nuts, and mini chocolate chips to cream mixture, folding twice.

Place in Cool Whip containers; freezing 5 hours or overnight.

M & M COOKIE BARS

1-1/2 cups, packed brown sugar
1-1/2 cups, softened butter
1 cup, quick cooking oats
1 cup, Rice Krispies
2 cups, all-purpose flour
1 tsp, baking soda
½ tsp, salt
35 each, Kraft caramels
½ cup, milk
14oz bag, M & M's

* 9x13 baking dish

Preheat oven to 350 degrees. Spray baking dish w/Pam or butter spray. Combine all ingredients in large mixing bowl; until blended. Pat 2/3 of mixture into baking dish. Bake for 10 minutes.

While baking, melt caramels w/milk in microwave.

Sprinkle 1 cup of M & M's over baked crust. Drizzle caramel over M & M's. Drop teaspoons of reserved dough on top and sprinkle w/1 cup M & M's, if desired.

Bake another 24 minutes. Remove from oven; letting cool 30 minutes.

MAJESTIC PUDDING

2 cups, soft bread crumbs
½ cup, milk
2 eggs, beaten
½ cup, packed brown sugar
½ cup, chopped beef suet
½ cup, all-purpose flour
½ tsp, baking soda
½ tsp, ground nutmeg
½ tsp, ground cinnamon
¼ tsp, salt
1 cup, finely chopped Honey Crisp apple
1 cup, raisins
¼ cup, mixed candied fruits and peels
½ cup, finely chopped walnuts
Foamy Sauce or Hard Sauce

Soak the bread in milk; beat smooth. Stir in eggs, brown sugar, and suet. Stir together flour, baking soda, spices, and salt. Add fruits and nuts; mix well. Stir in bread mixture. Oil and lightly flour a 1-quart mold. Press pudding into mold. Cover with foil; tie with string. Place on rack in deep kettle; adding boiling water 1 inch deep. Cover and steam 2 hours or until done.

Foamy Sauce: Beat 2 egg whites to stiff peaks; gradually add 1 cup sifted powdered sugar. Beat 2 egg yolks and ¼ tsp vanilla extract until thick; fold into egg whites. Whip ½ cup whipping cream to soft peaks; fold into egg mixture.

Hard Sauce: Thoroughly cream ½ cup butter or margarine with 2 cups sifted powdered sugar. Add 1 tsp vanilla extract w/1 beaten egg yolk; mix well. Fold in 1 stiffly beaten egg white. Chill.

MARBLED OREO CHEESECAKE W/RASPBERRY SAUCE

16oz cream cheese, softened
¾ cup, sugar
¾ cup, half and half
2 tsp, vanilla extract
3 eggs
2 Tbsp, un-sweetened cocoa
9" Oreo pie crust
10oz package, frozen raspberries, thawed, pureed and strained

In small bowl, blend cream cheese, sugar, half & half and vanilla until smooth. Beat in eggs 1 at a time.

Remove 1 cup batter; combining w/cocoa. Spoon half the chocolate batter over pie crust. Evenly pour white batter over chocolate batter. Top with spoonfuls of remaining chocolate batter. Cut through batter w/knife to create marbled effect.

Bake for 50 minutes. Cool completely. Chill 6 hours, serving w/raspberry sauce.

MARSHMALLOW MARBLE FUDGE

3-1/2 cups, Hershey's semi-sweet chocolate chips
6 Tbsp, butter or margarine, divided
14oz can, Eagle Brand sweetened condensed milk
2 tsp, vanilla extract
Dash of salt
1 cup, chopped nuts
2 cups, miniature marshmallows

* 9 inch square pan

Line pan w/foil; set aside. In saucepan over low heat, melt chocolate chips and 3 Tbsp butter w/sweetened condensed milk, vanilla and salt. Remove from heat; stirring in nuts. Spread evenly into prepared pan. In medium saucepan over low heat, melt marshmallows w/remaining 3 Tbsp butter. Pour over fudge. With table knife or metal spatula, swirl through fudge. Refrigerate 2 hours or until firm. Remove from pan; peel off foil. Cut into squares. Store loosely covered at room temperature.

Yield 5 dozen squares.

MOLASSES DROPPED BALLS

1 cup, butter or margarine
¼ cup, molasses
2 cups, all-purpose flour
2 cups, finely chopped walnuts
Powdered sugar

* Large cookie sheet

Set oven to 350 degrees. In mixer bowl, beat butter or margarine on medium speed of electric mixer for 1 minute. Add molasses and beat until fluffy. Add flour to butter mixture; beat a low speed until well blended. Stir in nuts; blend well. Using 1 Tbsp of dough for each, shape dough into 1 inch balls. Place on un-greased baking sheet, baking for 25 minutes. Remove from oven; cooling on wire rack.

When cookies are cool, gently roll in powdered sugar to coat.

MOUNTAIN DEW TURNOVERS

2 cans, crescent rolls
2 large, Honey Crisp apples, peeled and sliced
2 Tbsp, ground cinnamon
2 cups, white sugar
2 sticks, butter, softened
12oz can, Mountain Dew

* 9x13 cake pan

Preheat oven to 375 degrees. In small bow, mix cinnamon, sugar and butter. Unroll 1 can crescent roll and place in bottom of cake pan. Place apple slices in center of each crescent rolls. Put half of cinnamon mixture on apples. Top w/another can crescent roll; sealing edges together forming turnovers. Pour Mountain Dew around turnovers, not on top. Add remainder of cinnamon mixture over turnovers.

Bake for 45 minutes; letting cool at least 15 minutes before serving.

NEIMAN MARCUS COOKIES

3 cups, butter or margarine
5 cups, all-purpose flour
2 tsp, baking soda
2-1/2 cups, white sugar
6 cups, dry oatmeal
24oz bag, chocolate chips
2-1/2 cups, light brown sugar
1 tsp, salt
16oz Hershey Bar, grated
5 eggs, beaten
2 tsp, baking powder
2 tsp, vanilla extract
4 cups, pecans, chopped

* Large cookie sheet

Preheat oven to 375 degrees. Blend oatmeal in a blender to a fine powder. Blend the butter, and both sugars. Add eggs and vanilla; mixing together w/flour, oatmeal, salt, baking powder, and soda. Add chocolate chips, Hershey Bar, and pecans. Roll into balls and place evenly on un-greased cookie sheet.

Bake 10 minutes. Remove from oven; letting cool before serving.

Yield 10 dozen cookies.

NO BAKE PEANUT BUTTER BARS

¾ cup, packed brown sugar
½ cup, Caro Syrup
½ cup, peanut butter; crunchy or creamy
1 tsp, vanilla extract
2 cups, Rice Krispies cereal
½ cup, Cornflakes

ICING

¾ cup, packed brown sugar
¼ cup, evaporated milk
3 Tbsp, butter or margarine

* 11x7x2 inch pan

In saucepan, heat brown sugar and Caro Syrup over medium heat until sugar is dissolved. Stir in peanut butter and vanilla; mixing well. Fold in cereals. Spread into greased pan.

Combine icing ingredients in another saucepan; cook and stir over medium heat for 10 minutes, or until sugar is dissolved and icing has thickened slightly. Pour over bars; spread evenly.

Refrigerate 2 hours before cutting.

Yield 2 dozen.

NO MESS PIE CRUST

2-1/2 cups, all-purpose flour
½ tsp, salt
2 tsp, sugar
1/2 tsp, baking powder
½ cup, canola oil
1/3 cup, cold water

* 9 inch pie pan

Whisk together the flow, salt, sugar and baking powder.
Whisk together the oil and water; pouring over dry
ingredients. Stir w/fork until the dough is evenly moistened.
Pat dough across pie pan and up sides. Crimp edges; or
flatten tines w/a fork.

Fill crust as desired, and bake.

ORANGE JUICE PIE

1 can orange juice from concentrate
2 containers, cream cheese, softened
¼ cup, white sugar
12oz container, Cool Whip
9" baked pie crust

In a large bowl, mix orange juice and cream cheese until well blended. Fold in sugar and Cool Whip. Pour into pie crust.

Refrigerate 4 hours before serving.

OREO CHEESECAKE CUPCAKES

12 double stuffed Oreos
16oz container, cream cheese
½ cup, white sugar
½ tsp, vanilla extract
2 large eggs, beaten
½ cup, sour cream
½ tsp, salt
1/2 cup, hot fudge drizzle
18 cupcake liners

* Muffin tin

Preheat oven to 300 degrees. Line muffin tins w/cupcake liners. Place an Oreo in the bottom of each muffin cup. In a large bowl, beat cream cheese and sugar together until smooth. Blend in vanilla extract, eggs, sour cream, and salt. Continue beating until combined and smooth. Add heaping Tbsp of cheesecake batter to each muffin cup. Melt hot fudge drizzle in the microwave for 15 seconds. Place ½ teaspoon of hot fudge drizzle into each cupcake. Add another Tbsp of cheesecake batter on top; filling the cupcake liner. Use toothpick to gently swirl fudge into cheesecake mix.

Bake 30 minutes. Cool completely.

Keep in refrigerator, until ready to serve.

PEANUT BUTTER HONEY FRUIT DROPS

¾ cup, creamy peanut butter (crunchy, if desired)
¼ cup, butter or margarine, softened
3 eggs, beaten
½ cup, dark honey
½ cup, cold milk
2 cups, diced mixed candied fruits and peels
2 cups, all-purpose flour
½ tsp, baking powder
½ tsp, baking soda
½ tsp, ground cinnamon
½ tsp, ground nutmeg

* Large cookie sheet

Set oven to 350 degrees. Grease cookie sheet and set aside.
In a bowl, mix together peanut butter and butter until
blended. Stir in eggs, honey, and milk; blending well. Stir in
candied fruits and peels.

Stir together flour, baking powder, baking soda, cinnamon,
and nutmeg; gradually blending into candied fruit mixture.
Drop dough by teaspoonfuls 2 inches apart on cookie sheet.

Bake for 12 minutes or until golden brown. Remove from
oven; letting cool on wire rack.

PEANUT BUTTER STRIPED DELIGHT

35 Oreo chocolate sandwich cookies
6 Tbsp, butter, melted
8oz package, cream cheese, softened
¼ cup, white sugar
3 cups + 2 Tbsp, cold milk, divided
8oz container, Cool Whip, thawed and divided
2 boxes, Jell-O Vanilla instant pudding
1/3 cup, creamy or crunchy peanut butter, your choice

* 9x13 glass baking dish

Place cookies in food processor; covering and processing to fine crumbs. Transfer to medium bowl; add butter and mix well. Press firmly onto bottom of baking dish. Refrigerate 10 minutes. Meanwhile, beat cream cheese, sugar, and 2 Tbsp cold milk in separate bowl until well blended; adding ¼ cup Cool Whip, mixing well. Add dry pudding mixes; beating w/wire whisk 2 minutes. Add peanut butter; mix well. Spread evenly over cream cheese layer; letting to stand 5 minutes. Top w/remaining Cool Whip and cover.

Refrigerate 4 hours; makes 24 servings.

PEANUT CLUSTERS

4 boxes, white chocolate squares
1 box, German chocolate squares
1 bag, semi-sweet morsels
32oz jar, dry roasted peanuts, salted

* Crockpot

Melt all chocolate in Crock-Pot; add all contents from jar of roasted peanuts. Mix until well blended.

Remove contents 1 Tbsp at a time onto wax paper; making into clusters. Let set until no longer tacky to the touch.

Keep stored in large tightly covered bowl at room temperature.

PECAN PIE BARS

3 cups, all-purpose flour
½ cup, granulated sugar
1 cup, butter
½ tsp, salt
4 eggs, beaten
1-1/2 cups, light corn syrup
1-1/2 cups, white sugar
3 Tbsp, butter, melted
1-1/2 tsp, vanilla extract
2-1/2 cups, pecans, chopped

* 15x10 inch baking pan

Preheat oven to 350 degrees. Heavily grease baking pan; setting aside.

CRUST: Beat flour, 1 cup butter, ½ cup sugar and salt until mixture resembles crumbs. Press mixture firmly into baking pan; bake 20 minutes.

FILLING: Blend eggs, corn syrup, 1-1/2 cups sugar, 3 Tbsp butter and vanilla; until smooth. Stir in chopped pecans; spreading over crust.

Bake for 30 minutes or until set; cooling to cut into bars.

Yield 50 bars.

PECAN PIE COBBLER

1 box, refrigerated pie crust
2-1/2 cups, light corn syrup
2-1/2 cups, packed brown sugar
½ cup, melted butter
4 tsp, vanilla extract
6 eggs, lightly beaten
2 cups, chopped pecans
Butter cooking spray
2 cups, pecan halves
Vanilla ice cream for topping; optional, highly recommended.

* 9x13 inch glass baking dish

Set oven to 425 degrees. Lightly grease baking dish; set aside. Remove one pie crust from package, rolling out to fit the baking dish. Trim edges.

In large bowl, combine corn syrup, brown sugar, butter, vanilla and eggs; whisking until well combined, stirring in chopped pecans; spooning half of filling into crust.

Remove the second crust from the package, rolling out to fit baking dish, lightly spraying with butter spray; placing over filling.

Bake 16 minutes or until lightly browned; removing from heat.

Reduce oven temp to 350 degrees; carefully spooning remaining pecan filling over crust. Arrange pecan halves over top; baking 30 minutes. Let cool 15 minutes; serving w/ice cream.

POLKA DOT COOKIES

1 package, Devil's food cake mix
1/3 cup, canola oil
2 eggs, beaten
1 bag, white chocolate chips

* Large cookie sheet

Preheat oven to 350 degrees. Grease cookie sheet w/Pam spray. In large bowl, mix all ingredients until well blended.

Place on cookie sheet; baking 15 minutes.

Let cool; cutting into squares.

POTATO CHIP COOKIES

1-1/2 cup, white sugar
1-1/2 cup, light brown sugar
1-1/2 cup, butter or margarine
3 eggs, lightly beaten
2-1/2 cups, all-purpose flour
1 tsp, baking soda
6oz bag, butterscotch baking chips
2-1/2 cups, crushed potato chips

* Large cookie sheet

Preheat oven to 325 degrees. Mix butter or margarine, sugars and eggs until well blended. Add flour and soda, mixing well. Stir in potato chips and butterscotch chip; folding 2 times.

Drop on ungreased cookie sheet, 1 Tbsp at a time; baking for 18 minutes. Remove from oven; letting cook on wire rack.

Yield 4 dozen.

PRETZEL PINEAPPLE SALAD

1 cup, pretzels, crushed
½ cup, granulated sugar
1 stick, butter, melted
8oz package, cream cheese, softened
½ cup, granulated sugar
20oz can, crushed pineapple, drained
8oz container, Cool Whip

* Large cookie sheet

Preheat oven to 400 degrees. Spray cookie sheet w/Pam spray; set aside. In large mixing bowl; add pretzels, ½ cup sugar, and melted butter; mixing well. Place on cookie sheet; baking 7 minutes, letting cool. Break up into small pieces.

Mix together; cream cheese, ½ cup sugar; blending well, adding crushed pineapple, and Cool Whip.

Keep refrigerated.

Before serving, stir in pretzel crunch.

PUDDING GINGERBREAD MEN

½ cup butter or margarine, softened
½ cup, packed brown sugar
4oz package, butterscotch pudding mix
1 egg, beaten
2 cups, all-purpose flour
½ tsp, baking soda
1-1/2 tsp, ground ginger
½ tsp, ground cinnamon
2-1/4 cups, sifted powdered sugar
2 Tbsp, frozen lemonade concentrate, thawed
Water
Gumdrops and assorted other candies (optional)

* Large ungreased cookie sheet

Preheat oven to 350 degrees. Cream butter or margarine, brown sugar, and pudding mix. Add egg; beat well. Combine flour, baking soda, ginger and cinnamon. Stir into creamed mixture; chill.

Roll part of chilled dough out on floured surface to ½ inch thickness. Cut with 4 inch gingerbread-man cutter. Place on ungreased cookie sheet. Bake for 8 minutes; removing from cookie sheet, and letting cool.

Mix powdered sugar, lemonade concentrate, and enough water to make of spreading consistency. Frost gingerbread men or use pastry tube to pipe on frosting decorations.

Decorate w/candies, if desired. Yield 2 dozen cookies.

PUMPKIN APPLE CAKES

½ cup, butter or margarine
2 eggs
1-1/2 cups, white sugar
1-3/4 cup, all-purpose flour
1 tsp, baking soda
½ tsp, ground cinnamon
½ tsp, ground nutmeg
¼ tsp, salt
¼ tsp, ground cloves
¼ tsp, ground ginger
1 cup, canned pumpkin
½ cup, apple juice
1-1/2 cups, sifted powdered sugar
2 Tbsp, milk

* 8-1/2 inch fluted tube pan

Set oven to 350 degrees. Grease fluted tube pan; set aside.
Bring butter or margarine and eggs to room temperature.

In large mixer bowl, beat the butter or margarine until creamy
and fluffy. Gradually add the granulated sugar, beating at
medium speed for 8 minutes, or until light and fluffy; sugar
being dissolved. Add eggs, one at a time, beating 1 minute
after each egg; scraping side of bowl frequently. Stir together
flour, baking soda, cinnamon, nutmeg, salt, cloves, and
ginger. Add to creamed mixture alternately with pumpkin
and apple juice, beginning and ending with flour. Beat just
until blended. Turn batter into prepared pan; filling 2/3 full.
Bake for 50 minutes; removing from oven, letting cool 15
minutes. Turn onto wire rack; cooling completely. (See next
page for glaze.)

Stir together powder sugar and enough milk to make a glaze of drizzling consistency; spooning over cooled cakes

Yield 10 small cakes or 1 large cake.

QUICK BANANA PUDDING

½ cup, sugar
1/3 cup, all-purpose flour
3 egg yolks, beaten
2 cups, whole milk
2 Tbsp, butter, softened
2 tsp, vanilla extract
8 bananas, sliced
6oz box, Salerno Butter Cookies
2 tubs, Cool Whip

* 2.75 quart casserole dish

Layer bottom and sides of casserole dish w/butter cookies; set aside. In large mixing bowl; add sugar, flour, egg yolks, whole milk, butter, and vanilla extract; mixing until well blended. Transfer to medium sauce pan; heating on stovetop, stirring constantly until pudding has thickened.

Pour ½ of pudding mixture over cookies; adding ½ of bananas, and 1 tub of Cool Whip; repeating w/another layer.

Refrigerate for 5 hours before serving.

RHUBARB CAKE

1-1/2 cups, sugar
1 Tbsp, Crisco
1 egg
1 cup, sour milk
1 tsp, soda (mix w/milk)
2 cups, finely chopped rhubarb
2 cups, sifted flour
Dash of salt

* 9x13 cake pan, greased; set aside

Preheat oven to 350 degrees. In large mixing bowl; blend together sugar, and egg. Add sour milk w/soda; adding flour and blend. Stir in rhubarb; pouring into cake pan. Sprinkle w/cinnamon and sugar.

Bake for 35 minutes. Let cool completely before serving.

RITZ PEANUT PUFFS

2 sleeves, Ritz Crackers
Peanut butter to spread
1 bag, Campfire Marshmallows

* Large cookie sheet, ungreased

Preheat oven to 300 degrees. Place Ritz Crackers ½ inch apart on cookie sheet. Spread each cracker w/peanut butter; adding ½ Campfire Marshmallow on top.

Bake for 2 minutes; removing from oven, letting cool completely before serving.

ROCKY ROAD MARSHMALLOW BARS

1 box, chocolate cake mix
½ cup, butter, melted
1/3 cup, water
¼ cup, packed brown sugar
2 eggs, lightly beaten
1-1/2 cups, chopped pecans
3 cups, miniature marshmallows
3/4 cup, creamy chocolate frosting

* 9x13 cake pan, greased; set aside

Preheat oven to 350 degrees. In large bowl, stir together half of the dry cake mix, butter, water, brown sugar, and eggs until smooth. Stir in remaining cake mix, and pecans until well blended. Spread cake mix in greased cake pan; baking 25 minutes; sprinkle w/marshmallows.

Bake 15 minutes longer, or until marshmallows are puffed and golden brown.

In microwave bowl, microwave frosting uncovered on high 15 seconds. Drizzle over bars. Cool completely, about 2 hours. For easier cutting, use plastic knife dipped in hot water.

Yield 2 dozen bars.

SANTA'S COCONUT ROLLS

1 cup, butter, softened
1 cup, white sugar
2 Tbsp, milk
1 tsp, vanilla or rum flavoring
2-1/2 cups, all-purpose flour
¾ cup, finely chopped red or green candied cherries
½ cup, finely chopped pecans
¾ cup, flaked coconut

* Large ungreased cookie sheet

In mixing bowl, cream together butter and sugar; blend in milk and vanilla or rum flavoring. Stir in flour, chopped candied cherries, and pecans. Form dough into two 8-inch rolls. Roll in flaked coconut to coat outside. Wrap in waxed paper or clear plastic wrap; chill thoroughly.

Preheat oven to 375 degrees

Cut into ½ inch slices; placing on ungreased cookie sheet. Bake 12 minutes, or until edges are golden brown.

Yield 45 Whiskers.

SCOTCHAROOS

6 cups, Rice Krispies
1 cup, sugar
1 cup, light corn syrup
1 cup, peanut butter
6oz bag, chocolate morsels
6oz bag, butterscotch morsels

* 9x13 cake pan, well greased

In large saucepan, blend sugar, and light corn syrup; bringing to a boil on stove, adding peanut butter and Rice Krispies. Mix well, placing in cake pan.

In another saucepan, melt morsels together until blended. Pour over Scotcharoos; letting cool 2 hours before slicing.

SIMPLE BUTTERSCOTCH CAKE

1 box, yellow cake mix
2 eggs, lightly beaten
1 can, "Thank You Pudding", butterscotch
½ cup, light brown sugar
11oz bag, butterscotch chips

* 9x13 cake pan, lightly greased

Preheat oven to 350 degrees. Mix together cake mix, eggs, and pudding; blending well. Pour batter into cake pan and sprinkle w/brown sugar and butterscotch chips.

Bake 40 minutes, or until toothpick inserted in the middle come out clean.

SIMPLE CHOCOLATE CAKE

1 box, chocolate cake mix
2 eggs, lightly beaten
1 can, "Thank You Pudding", chocolate
½ cup, white sugar
11oz bag, chocolate chips

* 9x13 cake pan, lightly greased

Preheat oven to 350 degrees. Mix together cake mix, eggs, and pudding; blending well. Pour batter into cake pan and sprinkle w/white sugar and chocolate chips.

Bake 40 minutes, or until toothpick inserted in the middle come out clean.

SIMPLE WHITE CAKE

1 box, white cake mix
2 eggs, lightly beaten
1 can, "Thank You Pudding", vanilla
½ cup, white sugar
11oz bag, white chocolate chips

* 9x13 cake pan, lightly greased

Preheat oven to 350 degrees. Mix together cake mix, eggs, and pudding; blending well. Pour batter into cake pan and sprinkle w/white sugar and white chocolate chips.

Bake 40 minutes, or until toothpick inserted in the middle come out clean.

SOPAPILLA CHEESE CAKE

2 cans, thick crescent rolls
16oz container, cream cheese, softened
1 stick butter, melted
1-1/2 cups, white sugar
2 Tbsp, cinnamon
2 tsp, vanilla extract
2 each, 21oz cans favorite pie filling
2 small packets, chopped pecans

* 9x13 greased cake pan; set aside

Preheat oven to 350 degrees. Place 1 can crescent rolls in bottom of cake pan; sealing seams. Mix cream cheese w/1 cup sugar, and 2 tsp vanilla extract w/mixer for 1 minute or until well blended. Spread cream cheese mixture over crescent rolls. Spread both cans of pie filling over cream cheese mixture. Place 2nd can of crescent rolls over pie filling; sealing seams. Mix ½ cup sugar, and 2 Tbsp cinnamon together; shaking over 2nd crescent roll. Sprinkle 2 small packets of chopped pecans over top of cinnamon/sugar mixture. Pour melted butter over top of all ingredients.

Bake dessert for 45 minutes or until golden brown. Let cool completely before serving.

Keep refrigerated after serving.

SQUARE PRETZEL ROLOS

1 bag, square pretzels
1 bag, Rolos Caramel Chocolate candies
1 bag, pecan halves

* Large cookie sheet

Preheat oven to 350 degrees. Place square pretzels evenly in cookie sheet. Place 1 Rolo on top of each square pretzel.

Bake 5 minutes; removing from oven, and pressing 1 pecan halve lightly into top of Rolo candy.

Let cool, or put in fridge until cooled.

Put in airtight container at room temperature.

SUGARLESS PEACH PIE

8oz container, sour cream
1 small can, peaches, w/juice, chopped
1 small box, instant vanilla pudding mix, dry
1 baked pie shell or Graham Cracker crust
1 container, Cool Whip (if desired)

Mix sour cream, chopped peaches and dry pudding mix together; until well blended. Pour into pie shell; topping w/Cool Whip, if desired.

Keep refrigerated.

TAPIOCA PUDDING

3 Tbsp, tapioca
3 Tbsp, sugar
1 egg yolk
2 cups, whole milk
1 egg white
1 tsp. vanilla

In medium saucepan; stir 1 at a time, tapioca, sugar, egg yolk, and whole milk. Cook on low heat until thickened; removing from heat.

Stir in egg white and vanilla; blend well.

May be eaten warm or cooled.

TEXAS CHOCOLATE SHEET CAKE

2-1/2 cups, granulated sugar
2-1/2 cups, all-purpose flour
3/4 lb, butter, softened
1-1/4 cup, water
4 Tbsp, dry cocoa
½ cup, buttermilk
1 Tbsp, vanilla extract
2 eggs, beaten
1 Tbsp, baking soda

FROSTING

¼ cup, butter, softened
3 tsp, cold milk
2 tsp, dry cocoa
2 cups, Confectioners sugar
1 Tbsp, vanilla extract
1 cup, chopped pecans

* ½ Sheet cake pan; sprayed w/Pam spray, and set aside

Preheat oven to 350 degrees. Mix together sugar and flour; setting aside. Bring to a boil the butter, water and cocoa. Pour over flour mixture and stir. Add buttermilk, vanilla, eggs and baking soda. Mix well and pour onto sheet cake pan. Bake 20 minutes; letting cool until just warm, frost w/sheet cake frosting.

Frosting: Melt butter, milk and cocoa together. Remove from heat. Add powdered sugar, vanilla extract and chopped pecans. Beat well and spread on frosting while both cake and frosting are warm.

TOFFEE PECAN CARAMEL BUNDT CAKE

1-1/2 cups, unsalted butter, softened
2 cups, light brown sugar, packed
1 cup, granulated sugar
5 large eggs
3-1/2 cups, all-purpose flour
1 tsp, baking powder
½ tsp, salt
1-1/4 cup, whole milk
8oz bag, toffee bits
1 cup, chopped pecans
Non-stick butter spray
1 large bottle, caramel sauce

* Non-stick Bundt pan; spray w/butter spray, set aside

Preheat oven to 325 degrees. Beat butter until creamy, adding sugars. Beat until fluffy. Add eggs, one at a time, beating until just the yellow disappears after each egg. In a medium bowl, combine flour, baking powder, and salt. Gradually add flour mixture to butter mixture in thirds, alternately w/milk in between each third. Beat until just combined. Stir in toffee bits and pecans; spooning batter into prepared pan.

Bake until a toothpick inserted near the center of cake comes out clean, 80 minutes. You may need to cover the top of the cake w/foil near the end of cooking time to prevent excess browning. Let cake cool in pan 15 minutes; removing from, and let cool completely on a wire rack.

Spread caramel sauce over cake before serving.

TRI LAYER BROWNIES

1 cup, quick cooking oats
½ cup, all-purpose flour
½ cup, packed brown sugar
¼ tsp, baking soda
6 Tbsp, butter or margarine
¾ cup, granulated sugar
¼ cup, butter or margarine, melted
1oz square, un-sweetened chocolate, melted and cooled
1 egg, beaten
2/3 cup, all-purpose flour
¼ tsp, baking powder
¼ cup, whole milk
½ tsp, vanilla extract
½ cup, chopped pecans
2 containers, Fudge Frosting

* 11x7 inch baking pan, lightly greased; set aside

For bottom layer, stir together first 4 ingredients and ¼ tsp salt. Stir in 6 Tbsp melted butter. Pat in baking pan. Bake 10 minutes.

For middle layer, combine granulated sugar, ¼ cup butter, and chocolate; add egg. Beat well. Stir together 2/3 cup flour, baking powder, and ¼ tsp salt; add to chocolate mixture alternately with a mixture of the milk and vanilla, mixing after each addition. Fold in pecans. Spread batter over baked layer. Continue baking at 350 degrees for 25 minutes. Cool.

Spread with fudge frosting. Cut into bars. Top w/walnut halves, if desired.

YELLOW SWEET CAKE W/BUTTER CREAM ICING

CAKE

1 stick, butter, softened
1 cup, sugar
1 tsp, vanilla
2 large eggs, beaten
1-1/4 cups, self-rising flour
½ cup, buttermilk

* 9x13 glass cake dish, lightly greased

Preheat oven to 350 degrees. Add all ingredients to a medium mixing bowl; blending well. Pour into cake dish, and bake 30 minutes.

ICING

½ stick, butter
¼ cup, cold buttermilk
2 cups, Confectioner's sugar
1 Tbsp, Caro Syrup
1 tsp, vanilla extract
2 dashes, salt

In small saucepan, clarify butter; about 5 minutes, until golden brown. Mix rest of ingredients w/mixer; pouring into saucepan, bringing to a boil and thickened; letting cool completely.

After all is cooled; frost cake.

INDEX

PAGE 108 – SOUPS

PAGE 135 - CROCK-POT

Made in the USA
Columbia, SC
29 February 2020